I0896570

From Stalingrad to Italy – Von Senger's War

From Stalingrad to Italy – Von Senger's War

The German General Who Defied Hitler

Andrew Sangster

Pen & Sword
MILITARY

First published in Great Britain in 2025 by
Pen & Sword Military
An imprint of Pen & Sword Books Limited
Yorkshire – Philadelphia

Copyright © Andrew Sangster 2025

ISBN 978 1 03612 766 4

The right of Andrew Sangster to be identified as
Author of this Work has been asserted by him in accordance
with the Copyright, Designs and Patents Act 1988.

A CIP catalogue record for this book is
available from the British Library.

All rights reserved. No part of this book may be reproduced, transmitted, downloaded, decompiled or reverse engineered in any form or by any means, electronic or mechanical including photocopying, recording or by any information storage and retrieval system, without permission from the Publisher in writing. NO AI TRAINING: Without in any way limiting the Author's and Publisher's exclusive rights under copyright, any use of this publication to "train" generative artificial intelligence (AI) technologies to generate text is expressly prohibited. The Author and Publisher reserve all rights to license uses of this work for generative AI training and development of machine learning language models.

Typeset by Mac Style
Printed in the UK by CPI Group (UK) Ltd, Croydon, CR0 4YY.

MIX
Paper | Supporting
responsible forestry
FSC® C013604

The Publisher's authorised representative in the EU for product safety is Authorised Rep Compliance Ltd., Ground Floor, 71 Lower Baggot Street, Dublin D02 P593, Ireland.
www.arccompliance.com

For a complete list of Pen & Sword titles please contact

PEN & SWORD BOOKS LIMITED
47 Church Street, Barnsley, South Yorkshire, S70 2AS, England
E-mail: enquiries@pen-and-sword.co.uk
Website: www.pen-and-sword.co.uk
or
PEN AND SWORD BOOKS
1950 Lawrence Road, Havertown, PA 19083, USA
E-mail: uspen-and-sword@casematepublishers.com
Website: www.penandswordbooks.com

Contents

Acknowledgments

Over the years I have been very grateful to those who work and administer the various archives, and for the work of fellow historians with their various insights and perceptions.

However, I am exceptionally grateful to my wife, Carol Ann, for her incredible patience as I disappear into archives and rarely emerge from my Study. I am also grateful for the support and encouragement of my friend and colleague the Revd Dr Canon Peter Doll, Vice-Dean of Norwich Cathedral.

The Revd Dr Andrew Sangster
August 2024

Preface

In the study of archaeology large prizes can be discovered which not only paint a picture of the past, but this discipline provides insights into human activity, often challenging current thinking of what happened before the current generation came into existence. When the large item is removed, smaller and seemingly meaningless items often emerge, offering curious aspects of previous events and the nature of past human life. The world wars of the twentieth century are not that dependent on archaeology as they have been well recorded. However, re-examining documents and accounts often throws new light on even the recent past. In this study the author's attention was attracted by finding a German general who was a deeply committed Christian attached to the Benedictine Order and way of life, and simply did not fit the current image of the Hollywood German commander. The initial impression was that it was a postwar image with only flimsy authenticity. Further investigation revealed there was some truth in this curious figure, and thereby raises issues as to how a sensitive, well-educated intellectual from a traditional German background could serve the criminal Nazi regime, led by an evil and dangerous dictator. He was a man whom his enemies grew to respect, and even after the war the new West German Bonn government felt able to trust him. It was like digging up the remains of a dinosaur which presented a new picture of a sheer unexpected enigma.

Many field commanders are bound to remain unknown, except for the restricted circles of scholars and the aficionado. Yet their qualities matched, if not surpassed, those of their better-known superiors who made their way into the fame of battlefield glory. There are several examples. General Lucian K. Truscott, who was sent to the Anzio bridgehead to replace the disgraced General Lucas at command of the US VI Corps. In October 1944 Truscott was made army commander, less than one and half years after he had been given command of the US 3rd Division. General Sir

Brian Horrocks, divisional commander since March 1942, was given command of the XIII Corps in North Africa in July, serving under Field Marshal Montgomery. Wounded, he returned to the battlefield in August 1944 in Normandy, still serving under Montgomery, to take over command of the XXX Corps. Acknowledged as a good field commander who paid particular attention to the care of the men under his command, Horrocks would not become an army commander until after the war, when he briefly commanded the British Army on the Rhine.

There are similar cases in the German army, and one stands out more than the others: General von Senger und Etterlin. There are many reasons for taking a closer look at von Senger, whose ability and character should be greater than is normally portrayed. In 1943 he led the brilliant German evacuation from Corsica and Sardinia, which can be compared to the evacuation from Sicily in which he helped, consequently being given command of the XIV Panzer Korps. As such he fought at Cassino, even though his name was overshadowed by those of the commanders in charge of the defence of the town (1st Fallschirmjäger Division's commander Richard Heidrich), as well as by the name of Germany's most famous commander in Italy, namely Albert Kesselring. Although Kesselring oversaw the operations on the entire front, it was von Senger und Etterlin who was in charge on the crucial spot which has become world famous in the Italian campaign. He not only distinguished himself at Cassino but also in the battles which followed during the withdrawal to the Apennines and during the Gothic Line campaign. Like Horrocks, von Senger never rose to the command of an army, but his post-war career was quite different as their qualities were eventually realised.

Von Senger has left us a brilliant but little read account of his memoirs, and stands out as a commander with a personality which deserves this closer look. Not in the least because it tries to understand how this morally and Christian motivated man was clearly distant from the Nazi regime, which he nevertheless served to the best of his abilities to keep fighting a lost war. This is probably a question which makes von Senger not only a good commander, but also an interesting figure whose life is outlined in this book.

Dr Pier Paolo Battistelli (Italian Historian)

Foreword

This book is a study of a little-known German battlefield general whose life, especially during the Second World War, provides a picture of a curious almost unique person who normally one would not associate with military command, and especially not in Nazi Germany. For this writer he came to life some twenty years ago when visiting Monte Cassino Abbey, while walking the famous Gustav Line, and hearing a Catholic priest saying this man was almost saintly. At first it sounded as if he were being sarcastic, but this was far from the case, and to hear of a German general of the Nazi era who was described as a Benedictine Oblate almost came as a shock, especially when told he was always in their obituary prayers, as he had died in 1963.* This German general used to attend the mass in the Monastery, and the priest explained how he cared for the Abbey and for many Italians. What he did, he said, was nothing short of a miracle, and then smiling said that it was not sufficient for canonisation, because he was just a man working in an evil world and for a wicked tyrant. Later research indicated that this general was not that well-known, no biographies apart from a small and emotional book written in Italian. It seemed senseless pursuing the subject, because it felt like holding a jigsaw piece wondering where to place it in a completed picture.

Any sound historian is always wary of memoirs and autobiographies, and even some biographies fall into the trap of becoming hagiographies. Many of the personally written works are often based on the writer's need for self-justification, some come close to an apologia, but they are rare. Most of them are more like efforts to produce a form of self-adulation and many which are downright egotistical. Honest diaries are better, but they are few and far between, the best being that of the diary of the

* Although he is sometimes described as a Tertiary the correct title was probably an Oblate, a committed lay person to the Benedictine rule of life.

British General Alan Brooke, as it was so honest it caused him postwar problems when first published. The diaries of Goebbels and Ciano (Mussolini's son-in-law and Foreign Minister) are interesting but with their political background there is a constant need for caution. In the memoirs of the subject of this book there are a few things he omits to which attention is drawn, possibly because of his conscience. However, there is no sense of self-adulation, but plenty of personal angst because of whom he served, and the sense of hopelessness because he recognised that it was a war which he knew they could not, or even should not win. Despite it being defeatist talk it was one of his views he expressed at the time, a very unusual German general.

Introduction

General von Senger was never a senior German general, he was no Manstein, Rommel nor Rundstedt, and was best known for his corps command in Italy (XIV Panzer). Surprisingly, even though he was rated as a good battlefield general, he never made it to the upper echelons of Germany's highest commands. Most of his colleagues and virtually all military historians since have commended him for his battlefield knowledge, the way he exercised that command, his knowledge of tactics and strategy, especially in defence. He was known to be stable and trustworthy as a general, but whether his failure to rise to the top level of military command was because he was not rated suitable, or because of his attitude towards Nazi politics, or his known Christian adherence, or other factors proved impossible to ascertain. However, on reading his personal accounts, the views and comments by contemporaries and historians, some sensible speculation becomes possible.

It will become undoubtedly clear as his story unfolds that his claim to be anti-Nazi was not just postwar justification as with so many others, but he was genuine and his views were well-known during the war years, even having to return to Berlin on the excuse of receiving a medal he did not care about, but to attend an indoctrination course. Not helpful for him amongst the hierarchy of the Nazi regime was the knowledge that he was a dedicated Roman Catholic Christian who held strong moral principles, at times openly defying Hitler's orders not to execute Italian prisoners who had been ordered to switch sides. For many this defiance could have ruined their careers or even lead to their execution, but he remained untouched probably because of his growing reputation for being brilliant at defence and counterattack. However, it is known that the Nazi regime remained deeply suspicious of him, and all these features tend to indicate why he remained a straightforward battlefield general, and he was only given an army in the last minutes of the war.

It is a feature of history writing that historians differ not just in their approaches to their subject but in their views and interpretations. This can arise from such reasons as a nationalistic approach, the need to be seen as critical, an inbuilt personal bias, a means for selling their book, and a multitude of other reasons. On digging through the German, British and American archives there is not much material on him, and even in his important memoirs he uses a code on personal matters, even referring to his wife Hilda as 'P'. It struck this writer that his memoirs were not as self-serving, self-justifying, or egotistical as most of his contemporaries, but reasoned and full of angst for the suffering in which he was obliged to be involved. It also became clear on wider reading that most historians, when they mentioned him praised his military ability, but also his unusual personality. After the battle for France in which he outstripped Rommel in the race for Cherbourg, his war on the Eastern Front followed by the Mediterranean was a time of defence for the Germans. One historian described him as 'the man responsible for the whole front from the sea to the watershed of the Apennines ... a gentle hero, far from the Hollywood stereotype of a stiff, monocled, arrogant German general'.[1] One historian described him as 'An outstanding soldier and master of defence tactics', another described von Senger as 'the thoughtful and able tactician who had defeated Clark's every move on the Cassino–Garigliano front'.[2/3] His opponents recognised him as having a reputation 'as the best tactician of either side', a view shared by most who have studied and researched the battles in Italy from Cassino up to the northern region to the surrender.[4] It has been pointed out that at the fighting in the Gustav Line defence, 'he did this with a skill that in the postwar years earned him the plaudits of his former enemies'.[5]

It has also been noted that he was a realist and not frightened of expressing his opinions. He knew from his experience in the Stalingrad battle that the war could not be won by Germany. He 'was never given to premature optimism and often reminded his superiors of the casualties his units had suffered from artillery fire'.[6] The irony is that while most historians who have studied his contributions are generally in praise of this battlefield general, he is not well-known on the public front, and for most he remains an unknown figure. Even Second World War students on hearing his name mentioned ask who he was, and where did he fight.

His available photographs do not illustrate a handsome figure, almost a sinister looking person until a few pictures show him smiling when the whole persona seems to change. His own son, who became a German general for the postwar West German government described him this way:

> His face once seen was not easily forgotten: his high forehead, under black hair receding at 53, bisected by a prominent vein, and his great beak of a nose between deep-sunken eyes, gave him in profile the look of a hawk. In repose his face was austere, but when he smiled, as he often did, the effect was attractive; and his hands with their long fingers, with which he gestured eloquently, were those of a pianist. His daughter remembered especially the way her father carried his trim, athletic frame: he was quite different from the Prussian image. You would have to see him move, with that gentle grace, not at all stiff – more French really than Prussian.[7]

There remain major questions concerning von Senger, not least as to why a Christian orientated general, who clearly saw and hated the barbaric nature of the Nazi regime, should have served them in the first place. He was aware of the opposition and resistance to the regime, personally knew some of those involved, and who paid with their lives, but he kept well clear of the plans to overthrow the Führer. Many have raised this issue and there are some answers which make sense, but first it is necessary to unfold his life and activities, and this will be addressed in the final chapter.

After digging through the few archives which carry minimum sound material the writer decided the best approach was to use his memoirs, written in the 1950s, and first produced in German in 1960. It was not a matter of simply repeating them, but producing a commentary on what he did during his lifetime and as a battlefield general, supporting this with historical observations. This method not only paints the historical background but leads the reader into von Senger's thought processes. His life's experiences have much to offer even in the broadest terms, giving the reader an impression from von Senger's view of the German military 'race' through France, and the curious way a conquering German general was well received because of his fluent French, geniality, and warmth of character. Von Senger next described in clear terms the bitter fighting on the Russian front, the extreme weather conditions, and the sense of defeat. He was better known for his service in the Italian campaign, of dealing with the issues of the breakdown of the Axis following Mussolini's downfall, evacuating the islands of Sicily, Sardinia, and Corsica, and finally the bitter fighting around Cassino and a rear-defence as the German armies were pushed further north to final defeat.

From the military perspective his tactics in defence, which gained him a solid reputation are interesting, but also the unusual trait of a commander who cared for the morale of his troops, often meeting them on the frontline, ensuring their well-being as far as was possible under the circumstances. In Britain and America, the Italian campaign was often seen as a backwater war, with cynical comments about 'D-Day dodgers', but von Senger paints a clear picture of the bitter fighting in debris and destroyed buildings, as being similar to that experienced in Stalingrad. His experience with the Partisans is curious because for a variety of explored reasons he was never one of their targets, probably based on his care of Italian civilians, their churches, and his ability to speak Italian; he was even safe when he was the *de facto* commander of Bologna. While in Bologna, von Senger found the fascist Blackshirts more difficult than the partisans, and he had to work against the SS to expel a leading citizen (a professor of medicine) who was the main stalwart of the Italian fascists. He eventually had to surrender to General Mark Clark, stood as a witness in the war crime trial against General Dostler, spent three years in a PoW Camp in Wales which provided some interesting insights, before eventually returning to Germany. He first worked in education but soon returned to his soldierly role helping the new Bonn government in military matters. Because of his known recorded anti-Nazi position, he was well-received as an acceptable servant to the state.

The following chapters describe this unusual German general against the historical backdrop through which he lived, and in the final chapter there are hopefully some conclusions with which the reader will agree, that von Senger was an outstanding battlefield German general but was never a Hitler supporter.

Chapter 1

Von Senger, His Early Years

General Fridolin Rudolph von Senger und Etterlin was born 4 September 1891, not knowing that it was an unfortunate decade in which to be born, because it meant like most of his generation he would, if he managed to stay alive, face two major world wars. He was born in Waldshut-Tienge, generally known as Waldshut which was a well-known crossing area for many areas, not least Switzerland. He was born into a wealthy family carrying the title *von*, and he came from a Roman Catholic background. He was evidently intellectually highly gifted, at first studying classics in Constance (Konstanz), which is a university city on the western end of Lake Constance in south Germany, and then changed to studying Law in Freiburg, an independent city in the state of Baden-Württemberg in south-western Germany. He was a typical young man on the move with ambitions for his future, and it was also clear that he was gifted in languages. In the past his family had been mainly lawyers or political administrators spread between the Black Forest and Lake Constance, but in the turbulent years following the Napoleonic wars and Germany forming as a nation, they had tended to lose their wealth but generally still worked as lawyers. His father's influence tended to focus on duty to the state which would have a marked effect on the young von Senger, as did his mother's deep religious convictions. The other factors which would play a major role in his life he shared with most Germans, mainly the conflict of the Great War and the consequences of defeat.

At the end of 1910 he did his training year of what is called today 'conscription', learning to be a soldier in the Baden Artillery Regiment. In 1912 he was successful in applying for a Rhodes Scholarship to study in Oxford which he continued until the outbreak of war in 1914. His selection by Oxford clearly indicated his academic ability, as Rhodes's Fellows as they were known, have over the years produced some world leaders, one example being Bill Clinton, later an American President.

Cecil John Rhodes (Prime Minister of the Cape Colony from 1880–1896 and Rhodesia was named after him) established this scholarship, and he left instructions (1902) that his scholarship demanded 'that no student shall be qualified or disqualified for election on account of his race or religious opinions', (later the scholarship include females). It was originally intended to bolster the unity of English-speaking countries, and included Commonwealth countries, the USA, and Germany. Today it has a wider circumference, and it has long been recognised as an achievement in itself to be selected. It was noted that while in Oxford he attended the chapel at least twice a day, which was expected but not done by all. His Christian faith was from his youth deep and meaningful, as would later be observed while the Second World War raged around the battle of Monte Cassino where he was stationed for its defence against the Allied attack, attending the Mass whenever possible. As a young man he had associated himself with the Benedictine Order as a Layman, and some of his time had been spent on trips to 'Beuron and other Benedictine monasteries in Germany'.[1] He admitted that his time in Oxford had given him a 'cosmopolitan outlook on national customs and conditions', which probably made him more sympathetic later when occupying foreign lands. He also added that it helped him never make judgements on other people based on where they lived or their nationality. This in itself made the Rhodes foundation worthwhile. He had been a student for nearly eight years, had no specific plans for his future, but had been attracted to Oxford life, later noting that 'I grew fond of the regulated life in the old buildings. I lived in an atmosphere of the humanities, adorned by an element of luxury in the beautiful centuries-old gardens'.[2] His future was to take a different road from academic 'regulated life' as the Germany military demanded his presence. He learnt to speak English fluently with an American General in 1945 stating that he spoke in 'Oxford English'. He was fluent in French, and attended later a military course in Italian which was considered passable. There is no doubt that he was a highly intelligent and a gifted individual.

As soon as the 1914–18 Great War started, he was back in Germany, undergoing training with thousands of others, working their way through basic military training, and gone were his hopes for a peaceful future as a lawyer. After the training period he was selected to become a reserve officer in the Freiburg Field Artillery, moving from that city's university to one of its barracks. It was not long, given the attrition of this modern war that he was soon on active duty. He witnessed firsthand the terrible trench warfare which for many survivors was a stark lesson not only in the reality of modern war, but a lesson in the tactics and strategies involved. His powerful intellect would have discerned many lessons from this painful experience. It was undoubtedly his intellectual acumen and leadership qualities which after the war led to him being given a regular commission and selected to work with the new *Reichswehr*. He would later choose the Cavalry arm and soon was offered a staff post in the Army High Command.

However, the human element of sorrow and compassion was not lost, and in December 1917 he had been dismayed to hear his brother, a fighter pilot had been killed, and he was determined that his brother's corpse should not be left in a mass grave. Despite some formidable shelling by the British artillery, and having identified where the body was buried, he dug down into the mass grave, found his brother at the third level of corpses, dragged him out by his feet, took him back to his car sitting his brother's corpse beside himself as he drove to a safer place. To any reader of this escapade, risking his life for his brother's corpse, was a clear indicator that von Senger had high personal standards and a sense of determination.

As the war was drawing to its close, he met his future wife in Jenlain, a small French village in the north of France. Her name was Hilda Margaretha von Kracht, although in his writings he always referred to her as 'P' keeping his personal life as private as possible. Her father had been Lieutenant General Friedrich von Kracht (1844–1933). She was wearing the uniform of the Bavarian Red Cross when they met, and they eventually married on 2 December 1919. They had two children, first a son called Ferdinand (1923–1987) and a daughter Marina Josepha (1926–2017) who married an Italian Count in 1947. His son would become a General in the *Bundeswehr* after the Second World War and famous in his own right. His daughter in the postwar era travelled all the way across war torn Italy to see her father in a prison camp, but she missed him by days. In the Second World War he would pass through the same village again where he met his wife, recalling her as having 'hair curling over the brow beneath her cap, the face with its clear oval outline, the large eyes and likely mouth evocative of Marie Antionette'.[3]

He summarised the next few years in a brief statement: 'Then came two years of riding school in Hanover, transfer to the cavalry, and eleven years of quiet garrison life in the Cannstatt Cavalry Regiment. It was during these years he developed a deep love for horses, riding, and showjumping. He was happy working in the *Reichswehr*, not least because it provided an income in Germany where there was growing poverty and lack of money. One historian stated that von Senger was 'reluctant' to be a soldier and only did so for financial reasons.[4] However, his life's story seems to indicate that although he originally had different ideas for his future, the events of 1914–18 had turned him into a professional military man with a keen interest in strategy and tactics. From some accounts he appeared in these turbulent years to have taken part in tackling a communist uprising in Saxony. Like many people, including Germans, he had a lifelong distrust of communism, especially as it was developing in the Soviet Union, which most people knew was developing into a totalitarian version of true Marxism.

After a brief interlude in Hanover, where, in his capacity as aide-de-camp of a brigade, he had so little to do that he went to live in the country, but then was transferred to Berlin. As noted, he developed a deep interest in horses whom he loved, and he spent some time in showjumping. In Berlin he wrote, 'I toiled hard for four and a half years at the Cavalry Inspectorate, until I was assigned, in the autumn of 1938, the command of the Göttingen cavalry regiment', a well-known and traditional name.[5] He admired the way the Germans clandestinely rebuilt their military despite the restrictions of the Versailles Treaty, but later agreed that the isolation of the *Reichswehr* had made it a state within the state which had been a factor in the collapse of the Weimar Democratic Republic. He was pleased to note that as far as he could tell there was not a single Nazi amongst the officers in his regiment, having developed early suspicions of the Nazi Party. He knew many of his comrades wanted a return to the monarchy which in Germany would have been a form of totalitarian rule. It was ironic that his transfer to the Army High Command as a lowly grade-one staff officer happened at the same time as Hitler assumed power. In the 1920s he had passed the Staff College entrance examination but was regarded as too old to join the course. When he worked as Chief of Staff of the Cavalry Inspectorate, he had a wider view of what was happening from within the OKH, the *Oberkommando des Heeres* (Army Command). He was becoming aware of the Nazi regime with the murder and displacement of generals, especially after the Night of the Long Knives. He was also interested and involved in the debate surrounding tank warfare, and started his lifelong belief that as good as tanks were, it would be infantry who would win any conflict. He also had to adjust to the fact that his beloved horses would be replaced by mechanised vehicles. Working on General von Seeckt's theory, Hitler in 1938 worked on the principle of *Schnelle Truppen* (fast troops) and created a new service under the command of General Guderian.

Von Senger tended to stay out of politics and was not at a senior enough level to know all that was being planned. He had no idea that Hitler and Stalin had reached an agreement over Poland (Molotov-Ribbentrop Pact) on 23 August 1939, with the secret protocol of planning the dividing of Poland between the two powers. At first, he regretted he took no part in the Polish campaign, even wondering if his military career was stalling or being put aside. He learnt from others about the disconcerting and appalling atrocities committed in Poland, especially by the SS.

Chapter 2

The Second World War

France

Von Senger wrote his war memoirs during the 1950s decade, and they were published in Germany in 1960. As will be noted later many foundations for this work were prepared in his postwar prison days when he was asked for reports and observations, and later when working for the Bonn governed in the early 1950s. Historians are always alert to the hidden agendas in postwar memoirs, aware of the self-justifications by those trying to distance themselves from the Nazi regime. Even on the Allied side some memoirs reflect similar traits but by trying to enhance their reputations or seeking some form of self-justification. In his war memoirs von Senger makes many references to his distaste of Hitler and later the regime, mentioning some of the military officers who started the German resistance; although it is possible that he knew what was happening, he was never an active participant. However, he was accepted back into postwar West Germany as an active component, and the Allies never considered putting him on trial. As his story unfolds the reader must be able to take his own views on General von Senger from his actions and reactions to the war as it unfolded. He is certainly a curious figure when placed alongside the traditional characteristics of his better-known contemporaries.

He took no part in the invasion of Poland, and although the German army used many horses for pulling guns and carts, von Senger recognised that in war cavalry, to use his own words, horses had become 'an anachronism'. The cavalry had transformed into mobile armoured warfare, and he was on the move with his regiment into the low countries, then France. Some of his and other officers' favourite horses were brought up in the rear so he could relax with them by being in the saddle. He often recalled his wife hunting side-saddle according to the English style. Later he recognised that the horses he and other officers took with them in the Second World War were 'luxurious toys of a declining era', recalling their names and characteristics with deep affection.

In his memoirs he referred to his batman Feuerstak whom he described as a quiet man who kept himself to himself and spent plenty of time either sitting quietly meditating or reading the Bible. This observation by von Senger either indicated how he appreciated this approach, or the batman was doing what he thought would endear him to his boss. Either way, from the opening passages of his memoirs it is clear that von Senger always took his Christian faith with him.

After Poland with a likely major war on their hands, von Senger wrote about other officers with whom he talked, concerned about their uncertainty of a 'showdown with the West' and their 'instinctive aversion to the Government we had no faith in', because the memory of the First World War was disturbing.[1] He then mentioned men like General von Hammerstein who resigned the moment Hitler came to power, and General Beck who was the focus of resistance to later assassinate Hitler (20 July Plot 1944), and many others related to the German resistance. At this stage von Senger had heard about some of the many atrocities committed in Poland, but he does not mention this, but more the sense of concern that the Germans were taking on the Western powers, whom they saw as more powerful. He also noted there were those officers who had no interest in politics but were merely concerned about military success, whom he referred to as 'politically uneducated', and who suited the Nazi regime. There were many others who appeared later from the Hitler Youth who were inspired Nazis, but in 1940 their numbers were not as numerous as they would soon become. It is difficult if not impossible to gauge whether von Senger had added these lines with the benefit of hindsight, and it is necessary to read his whole account to understand the man and give him the benefit of the doubt.

Von Senger mentioned he admired the Prussians who had always been regarded as soldiers who obeyed orders, not involve themselves in politics and obey their government. However, von Senger was political, disliked the current Nazi government, and he would later refuse some of Hitler's orders. It may be that he was reflecting on the more romantic views of past times, or there may have been a time when he felt the same way, until he saw Nazi instructions of obedience. This would be true of many nations where military obedience is taken for granted, and it would take the Nuremberg Trials of 1945–46 to raise questions of obeying all orders. Given these circumstances, von Senger was caught by surprise and wrote that 'it was all the more of a shock to me when on the evening of 9 May 1940, the executive order was issued for the invasion of neutral Holland [Netherlands]'.[2] In the February of this year Major General Baron von Waldenfelds had died from a stroke, and von Senger had moved up to command the 2nd Cavalry Brigade but no horses, all mechanised and was known as *Motorised Brigade von Senger* throughout the French occupation. He missed his horses writing that 'I realised that I had reached a turning point in my life; that without horses I would never be the same again. It was over! I reflected on my military past and the part horses had played in it'.

Having been given an 'executive order', there was no question for any soldier, even one with doubts, of anything except obedience. He also had the honesty, which often 'glows' when found in personal memoirs as it is unusual, namely the feeling of being confronted with the uncertainties of fate, adding that 'maybe it was just fear'. Such admissions help give his account a sense of integrity. He admitted that at one stage when confronted by Dutch fire he hid behind a tank which he knew was a mistake as a tank attracted most serious attacks, but the enemy raised a white flag, and thus begun for him and other surprised Germans the rapid collapse of the West. Later, near the Dutch town of Stavoren (West Frisian) which he approached on Whitsunday [Pentecost] he again admitted he 'cowered' behind a pile of bricks. His use of the word 'cowered' being closely associated with 'coward', again is unusual in its frank honesty about personal fear. It may well be unique that of all the German memoirs written of the Second World War it is only von Senger who offers the Church's liturgical calendar for his timing, and very few in the heat of battle would know or care whether it was Good Friday or even Easter. When they returned to their barracks von Senger noted they were greeted by the people with enthusiasm, noting that he was consumed with pain and compassion 'for the ignorance of those who had been misled'. Again, the question must be asked as to whether he really felt this or was it a postwar adjustment. These questions arose in the writer's mind when he first read Senger's book while at university in the mid-1960s, but the decision must wait for the last chapter, *Final Observations*.

By the end of May 1940 his brigade was to the south of Brussels where he saw the refugees from that city fleeing. Undoubtedly like many other senior and elderly officers he recognised areas he had traversed during his time in the First World War, seeing the place as the 'roads of war'. He had travelled the roads as a lieutenant and was doing it again as a Brigade commander. He even made small detours for the sake of memory, even finding in Jenlain the house where he first met his wife, Hilda. He was jerked out of his reminiscences by coming across what he described as the 'gruesome spectacle' of people linked by common misfortune. He described their pain and suffering, especially for the old and children, while many memoirs simply note the roads were packed with refugees. He paused at Vimy Ridge, which had been a scene of prolonged and bitter fighting in the First World War, noting that this time they were merely passing by and having to fight their way through. On arriving at Cambrai, he was told his newly formed brigade was to be known as the 'Von Senger Brigade', (*Von Senger Schnelle* [Fast] *Brigade*) which was the time when he felt his 'stage-fright' had evaporated, and while the Brigade was being assembled, he drove near to the frontline to see what was happening. His new brigade was intended to operate under Panzer Corps Hoth (General Hermann Hoth, later convicted as a war criminal) which had made its way as far as Rouen. To show the speed of advance by the Germans, von Senger noted they covered some 200 kilometres in 25 hours. They were attacked by British bombers and his adjutant drove through a minefield and was killed. Von Senger had the sad task of informing his adjutant's father, a fellow officer, who now had no sons left, and was evidently badly upset by the incident. After enjoying a rest and revisiting the sites he knew of old, his brigade was ordered to move toward Le Havre, which proved a straightforward exercise as the British troops had already escaped across the Channel. French oil supplies were in flames, there was widespread looting, poor water supplies, and hundreds of English lorries blocked the streets. Von Senger's sense of romantic war conducted by gentlemen was shattered when he realised that 'some of our own troops' waved a white flag [of surrender] only to use it to gain the initiative by capturing the French troops prepared to listen, or by using the trick to march through some areas without opposition, which von Senger regarded as an 'act of degeneration'.

In his memoirs von Senger took time to reflect on the deceased General von Seeckt and gave him credit for the speed of the German advance. He described his work during the interbellum years of combining air and tank power combined with infantry advances to gain surprise and speed of advance, this was later dubbed as Blitzkrieg. Later in Italy, von Senger would work under Field Marshal Kesselring who had worked closely with von Seeckt, and there was no doubt that von Senger's insight about Seeckt was accurate. The military historian Liddell Hart argued that although Seeckt died three years before the war, and retired ten years before that, he remained the single German General who had the greatest influence on the Second World War.[3] Von Senger must have been aware that under Seeckt's guidance the German government ignored the Versailles Treaty by rebuilding its forces and cooperating with the Soviets. The British were alert to the German-Soviet agreements and interchange of personnel; there must have been an awareness of German developments, but not necessarily intentions.* Von Senger specifically mentions his relationship with John Dill who later succeeded Ironside as CIGS, and it was not unusual for military personnel to be acquainted with their opposite numbers as Kesselring was with Winterbotham, the British air-attaché in Berlin, though he was really working for MI5.[4]

However, as far as von Senger was concerned the German military had been restored, and either at the time or with the benefit of hindsight, noted that France had swiftly fallen because of the work during the interbellum years, but with the British escape from Dunkirk it was not the end of the war. He recognised Britain's supremacy at sea, that she had colonies and Commonwealth in support, and having studied in Britain claimed he knew the British believed 'they fought for an ideal that could not be understood by the Germans under the Hitler regime'.[5] He referred to the British understanding and belief in democracy, and this may well have been his thinking at the time, otherwise he may have

* Major Desmond Morton in the British Intelligence Service used to report on arms in other countries. He was a friend of Winston Churchill. Martin Gilbert, *Winston Churchill: The Wilderness Years* (London: Macmillan, 1981), p.15.

added that the democratic link with the USA transpired to be a major input into Allied victory.

After ruminating upon these matters, von Senger received orders from Rommel's 7th Panzer Division to head towards the important port of Cherbourg where there was reported opposition. Von Senger's Brigade was under Rommel's direction and ordered to approach the port from the direction of Valognes. Von Senger drove ahead in his car to view what was happening in the vicinity, where he heard the 7th Division had met resistance to the west of the city (19 July), so his brigade was to attack from the east. Taking his car von Senger moved with his column into Cherbourg with little opposition, although a bullet just missed him. On reaching the town centre he saw a statue of Napoleon on his horse pointing towards England, with his ironical thought of 'then as now'. The main problem was mopping up the prisoners who had to be removed from the peninsula. He also gathered that Rommel was peeved that the von Senger Brigade had arrived first, and as one historical account noted von Senger 'had bested the great Erwin Rommel in the race to capture the port of Cherbourg'.[6] He was ordered to move to Valognes having first joined some naval prisoners of war for a meal.

On arrival he met the mayor of Valognes and had a peaceful time discussing the immediate future with the town council, describing it as 'an enjoyable hour of office-work'. Having a meal with naval prisoners and a peaceful time with the Town Council was to become characteristic of von Senger. His known minor German nobility, his ability in foreign languages, his sense of friendliness and concern, all stood in stark contrast to the anticipated stiff monocled image of the traditional German officer of rank. This hallmark was noted by many during the war and often repeated in the postwar era. He heard the armistice was underway and so enjoyed a car ride through Normandy, amazed at the high hedges blocking his view. This typical feature of the landscape (known as bocage) would later in 1944 cause problems for the invading Allied troops on D-Day Normandy. He drove to Barfleur (a small fishing village) and was the first German to arrive. The people looked nervous, but they soon calmed down when von Senger spoke to them in his fluent French, and he enjoyed the sense of normality in the place.

Following orders, he took over the local administration at Rennes, which was packed with refugees trying to return home, but they were not allowed into the coastal zone, so camps were established. He found himself attending town council meetings again, which he found a busy time, but was pleased when his horses were brought to him so he could relax. Sitting in a café enjoying a meal and surrounded by civilians doing the same, some military patrol warned the diners to leave, and the military could stay until nearly midnight. Von Senger invited them to join his table so they could enjoy the evening. They sat there until midnight, mainly talking about politics. If this story is true, and it seems highly likely that von Senger was recalling a happy memory, it is a clear sign that his humanity came ahead of his military status or any sense of self-importance. He travelled to St Malo which he had visited in peacetime, meeting the owner of the hotel where he and Hilda had spent some holiday time. The proprietor even asked von Senger to convey his best wishes to his wife. Again, the conversation tended to be political around the dining table, with one French person saying the Germans had an efficient government, whereas they only had 'flabby Daladier' (French Prime Minister). They also felt the British had betrayed them by leaving Dunkirk, that they were never liked in that area of France, a French person stating that the German troops behaved better than the British, and he asked von Senger questions about National Socialism (The NSDAP was the Nazi Party). The Italian historian Giuseppe Trulli noted that this view of German soldiers was helped because von Senger's soldiers were well behaved under his command. It is a curious thought that at this moment in time the French civilians were enjoying the company of a civilised and accommodating German officer who spoke colloquial French, but in the following years the Nazi regime would show its true colours, and four years later the French would be rushing to greet the British and American troops invading Normandy.

Von Senger then had to find accommodation, a billet for himself and his immediate staff. He looked at various possible chateaux but while finding the occupiers pleasant and polite, he could sense they were not happy about him as a guest. He could have made use of the 'billeting regulations' which offered no choice, but evidently sensitive to the situation he continued until he found someone prepared to cooperate. While there he heard from his wife Hilda who had cried on hearing church bells announcing the defeat of France, but he deduced they were tears of sorrow and not joy, causing him to ruminate on the 'barbaric anti-Semitism' and reflecting on the many Jewish friends he once had. He asked himself as to 'how could the German people be led along such a wrongful path?'[7] As a widely travelled person with a cosmopolitan outlook he must have known that anti-Semitism was widespread in Europe, even in France and England, so he must have been aware of the added cruelty of the Nazi regime towards Jews to raise this question. In his hometown of Göttingen the local synagogue had been burnt to the ground during Kristallnacht, 9 November 1938, which he would have known about.

While sequestered in the peaceful French countryside he also reflected on the unexpected speed of the French defeat. He once again observed the German combination of forces as mentioned above with the work of von Seeckt. He realised the French had squandered their forces based on the Maginot formula with no means of a mobile defence force, and he understood why the British had made the decision to retreat to their island home. Now, he noted, the French armaments industry was working hard for German demands, which was to offer Hitler the resources he needed for further expansion plans.

Italian Liaison Officer

Typically, von Senger's memoirs are not a day-by-day account of his life at war but being an intellectual and sensitive to the judgements of history, he often paused to reflect on the nature of what happened and the consequences, not just from the military point of view, but the political angle as well as moral considerations. In July 1940 he was instructed to function as the liaison officer between the Franco-German and Franco-Italian commissions. He was undoubtedly given this post because his sound intellect had long been recognised.

As he travelled to his home in Göttingen (north central Germany, a university city in Lower Saxony) he saw part of his brigade still on their horses and stopped, not so much as to greet the men but pat the horses he so much loved. He reflected that in the new modern war he would not be riding them again, and he felt the pain by the loss of their company.

He arrived in Turin at the end of July 1940 for his work as a liaison officer. He knew Italy and had travelled it before and in 1938 had been there as part of a military mission. He had reached a series of decisions about what he termed Germany's partner (the *Axis*), including the Italian political scene. He regarded the link which Mussolini had created with the monarchy as a mere façade, but accomplished because the monarchy was deeply rooted in the Italian mind, even giving the appearance, he argued, that fascism had supported the monarch. Von Senger acknowledged that the Italian system was not as tainted as the Nazi regime, and again this has to be questioned whether he wrote this with the benefit of hindsight, but many others felt the same, including Churchill at one time. In the 1930s the British and French had a growing suspicion about the German government under Hitler, not helped by the fact that there had been the Great War. They regarded Italy under Mussolini in a different light because Italy had changed sides and joined the Western Allies, and although there existed a distaste of totalitarianism there was some hope that it appeared more civilised in Italy, and both the French and British wooed Mussolini in the hope that he would help stave off a German alliance.

Von Senger's memoirs spend little time on the precise nature of his work with the armistice commission, but he wanders off into several pages of reflection about how Italy and its alliance with Germany developed and all the ensuing problems. During this time in Italy, he noted the cracks appearing in fascism and the problems between the two dictators to reach firm conclusions on war issues. At times he wondered if he were expected to solve some of these issues. He noted that Italian soldiers were the same as in any other nation, which was sound common sense, and he spotted similarities between Prussians and the Piedmontese nobility, claiming he gained these insights while working for the Armistice Commission. He noted that in the Franco-German armistice commission in Wiesbaden they had requisitioned the whole hotel, but in Italy they occupied rooms along with the public, which von Senger preferred. Von Senger was there for a prolonged period of time and his wife Hilda at first could not join him because of strict travel restrictions, but the OKH (Army High Command) intervened, and she joined von Senger in the autumn of 1940.

He noted a change in Italian attitudes, believing it was based on their successful conquest of Abyssinia in 1936 and now their last-minute joining Germany against France. Von Senger felt they were 'sitting on their high horse', yet the German military knew the Abyssinian tribal opposition had been weak against a mechanised force, and they were not impressed with the Italian army's deficiencies. He was also aware that Mussolini's son-in-law and Foreign Minister Ciano was working for peace, looking more to England and France. He was accurate in this estimation as later Ciano's personal diaries would not only reveal this factor, but also his deep distaste for the Nazi regime and its various leaders. Ciano had had many talks and confrontations with the British during the 1930s over commercial negotiations regarding weapons, causing disquiet among financial experts, not least because the British deals amounted to 20 million pounds sterling in arms alone.[8] However, it was evident to Ciano and others that Mussolini was veering towards the Nazi regime, with Mussolini telling Ciano that 'governments are like people and must follow a line of morality and honour'.[9] Ciano's dislike and lack of trust in both the German and Italian regimes would later lead to his execution.

The Italians had been concerned over the German invasion of Poland, but they had greedily joined the Germans against France when it was clearly safe, and they were now making intolerable demands on the French at the armistice proceedings. The popular press was demanding the return of Corsica, Tunisia, and Djibouti (north-eastern coast of Africa), with even Ciano noting in his diary that the Corsican people now saw themselves as French.* There were, von Senger noted, glaring discrepancies between Italy's demands on France and the minor role Italy had played in the conflict. Von Senger suggested with sound insight that Hitler was more interested in what Vichy France could offer than Italy. As soon as Vichy France became a temporary reality the British perhaps more than the Americans, realised the danger of Admiral Darlan the politician as a potential enemy; he was considered to be more dangerous than Pierre Laval, 'partly because he was the more respectable politician and partly

* Monelli (a journalist friend of Ciano) returned from Corsica warning there were no irredentist feelings in Corsica. In 1767 the Republic of Genoa sold Corsica to France, ceding all rights in the 1768 Treaty of Versailles. It was incorporated into the French State in 1789 and by this time the population felt they were French.

because of his feelings of bitter animosity towards the British'.[10] Darlan, once claimed 'if we collaborate with Germany…that is to say, if we work for her in our factories, if we give her certain facilities, we can save the French nation; reduce to a minimum our territorial losses in the colonies and on the mainland; play an honourable, if not important role in the future Europe'.[11] Von Senger perhaps did not know at the time that Hitler had seen in some of the Vichy leaders a potential allied nation, as France had more in resources to offer than Italy. It was clear that Mussolini did not want Italy to be seen as a second-class power, but Italy lacked the natural resources for a major war, and in the meantime, Hitler hoping for a cooperative from Marshal Pétain in Vichy France was seeking French cooperation, even allowing them to keep their fleet, some armed.

Mussolini later attacked Greece through their client state of Albania only to fail and be rescued by the Germans. It was the same picture in North Africa when the well-known Rommel came to the Italian rescue, which gave more impetus to Hitler wanting to normalise some form of relationship with France because it was recognised that Italy was a weak partner. When Hitler decided to invade Russia (Operation *Barbarossa*) the Italians, namely Mussolini were astounded, and later Ciano would have the temerity to suggest peace with Russia to Hitler. Nevertheless, wanting to be seen as a great leader Mussolini later sent troops to the Russian front, which von Senger noted was a lost war from 7 December 1941 when the German army was repulsed at the very gates of Moscow.

Von Senger's stay in Italy appeared to be that of a military office manager, working between different functionaries, preparing various reports, and connecting with the various major figures in Italy. It was a lengthy task but in September he was promoted to Major General. He had probably been selected for this post because he was not a major military figure, but known as an intellectual, a diplomatic gentleman, and linguist. However, with problems appearing on the Eastern Front he was called away in the autumn of 1942 from what was regarded as a friendly backwater to the urgency of the Russian war, admitting 'I will not deny that I was impatient to be in the fray. There is something that compels the military man to "stick to his guns"'.[12] The Oxford Rhodes' scholar who had hoped for an academic or legal career had transformed not just into a soldier during the Great War, but 28 years later saw himself as a military man doing his duty, even though, according to his memoirs, he felt disgusted by his Nazi masters.

The Eastern Front

Of all the various memoirs written postwar by military figures, von Senger's work tends to be the most reflective both from a personal and political viewpoint. One of the curious features of his account is that he barely mentions his rank which he rose to slowly and remained a minor general, albeit becoming well-known later in the German defence of Italy. It was only on 1 September he progressed to Major General, and his progress can be seen in the form on page 8 of the plate section of this book, extracted from the German archives.

He left Italy for his hometown of Gottingen with his wife Hilda and his faithful military servant Feuerstak, reflecting on the lessons he had learnt from the trench warfare of 1914–18, where strategic issues were more controlled by the necessity of prompt operational decisions. He made a comment on the rise in ranks of other officers, noting the emergence of a new type who had no political concerns, had faith in the regime and were always enthusiastic. He reflected on the fact that men like Beck, who had a conscience, were becoming rare. Up to this point in his memoirs he made no mention of the cast of the fanatical Nazi generally found in Himmler's SS. By offering these insights, he raises again the issue which will permeate this study of why he continued in his military role under the Nazis whom he appeared not to trust. He spent a few days in the school for armoured troops, which given the previous months of office work in Italy was probably very sensible. He noticed the various differences between those instructors 'who had been in the fighting were evidently still affected by the Russian T-34 tanks and the withdrawals on the central front during the bitter winer of 1941/2'.[13] Others appeared less concerned, but von Senger was soon to find the realities of the Russian war as Commander of the 17th Panzer Division (originally the Augsburg Division) as he joined in the fruitless attempt under General Hoth to relieve General Paulus' Sixth Army at Stalingrad. Having control of a Panzer Division in these circumstances he knew would be a novel experience, but von Senger, being a studious if not fastidious man, had made a point of studying their tactics, and carefully listened to such discussions when at the OKW. Later he would cleverly and carefully cover the rear of Hoth's army and was awarded the Knight's Cross for gallantry.[14]

Very soon he drove to Berlin with his wife and batman Feuerstak, of whom he was very fond, and as he left to travel East, he admitted that it felt like 'falling into a huge dark chasm'. He travelled via Smolensk to the headquarters at Orel which took a week signifying the vast geographical expanses in the Russian campaign. Curiously, he had a private meal with the Army Commander, which gave him the impression that the privacy was because von Senger's political views were known about. He soon gathered from their conversation that many of the senior military officers felt the war could not be won, despite the encouragement and enthusiasm of the Nazi regime. It was a two-hour meal, and the Army Commander told von Senger to forget all they had spoken about over lunch. By this stage everyone had to keep personal thoughts to themselves or with highly trusted friends. This was true in the civilian world but also in the confines of the military sphere, it was all too easy to be accused of being a traitor even by expressing the slightest doubt about Hitler or his so-called military genius. Later, after the 20 July 1944 Plot, many thousands would be executed, many of them simply because they had the wrong friends.

In Russia the reality of war was epitomised for him when he took part in the attempt to relieve Stalingrad, and after the shattering defeat he had no illusions about the outcome of Hitler's war. It was von Senger's task to meet his 17th Panzer Division in the area southeast of Orel (sometimes known as Oryol or Oriel situated on the Oka River) which he found to have problems as it had no armoured cars, nearly half the trucks needed repairing, meaning that one company at least would have to travel on foot. There were only thirty tanks and von Senger wondered whether this appalling state was because of the sense of frantic hurry or sheer corruption. There seemed little doubt that there was a genuine and understandable sense of panic as it was already mid-December, and three weeks before the Russians had won the battle by surrounding the Sixth Army in Stalingrad where the most bitter fighting was taking place under the most appalling freezing conditions. This writer can recall playing chess with an old soldier who had fought in Stalingrad and always insisted on sitting near a radiator even in the summer. As he travelled, he met the commander of the Romanian Division, a seemingly embarrassing meeting as the Romanians had been defeated, and like other German allies such as the Italians and Hungarians were unhappy about being there in the first place. Von Senger's men had to march through deep mud, and he drove for twelve hours and still failed to reach his goal of the Colonel-General Hoth. When he telephoned Hoth he was told that they had to move faster in order to rescue the forces in Stalingrad, but von Senger pointed out that Hoth should be aware of the lamentable state of his men's equipment. General Hermann Hoth was later regarded as an efficient panzer commander, but he was a staunch Nazi and was later tried as a war criminal and given a prison sentence of 15 years. The current strategy was based on Manstein's plan to build a corridor towards the Sixth Army (Operation *Winter Storm*) to keep it supplied, and as such had Hitler's support, but because of pressure it had to be abandoned just before Christmas of that year.

Once there it struck von Senger that the German forces were physically inadequate for resisting the Russian strength, who were not only close by, and yet his force was some 60 miles away from Stalingrad. It was an 'impossible situation', von Senger wrote, and not with the benefit of hindsight. Paulus and his men had been ordered to stand and fight by Hitler, and Paulus an obedient servant did that, even though short of food, ammunition, nearly frozen to death, yet they knew their end was in sight. It was not surprising that when the much-vaunted Field Marshal Paulus was made prisoner (Hitler having made him a Field Marshal in the closing days, to encourage him to commit suicide as no German Field Marshal had ever surrendered) he publicly turned against the Nazi Regime. The men at Stalingrad also knew that such were the logistical strengths of the Soviets that even an attempt to break out would be suicidal. Göring had promised the impossible in airlifts as he had no concrete knowledge of the circumstances, and Hitler had personally contacted Paulus informing him all would be well.

Von Senger was further appalled when he realised the 23rd Division was even more badly equipped than his own, and he could see that the weakness of the proposed German attacking forces was so obvious that it was clear the Germans simply did not have the necessary reserves. In his memoirs on the Russian campaign, he lists many pages of his initial task which was to attempt a surprise attack on a place called Generalov and establish a bridgehead, a place supposedly free of the enemy but heavily mined. The problems emerged at once, not least the thaw had made the roads virtually impassable and a serious shortage of fuel, and having to set off at five in the morning on 17 December 1942. The next day it was a matter of reinforcing the new bridgehead, but von Senger had inadequate reserves to accomplish this issue, and the limited time meant armoured forces could not be used, which was not helped when the Panzer section's commander took the wrong route. In addition to these problems, the sheer freezing conditions of minus 20–25 made it impossible to refuel the vehicles, and in the icy conditions their grip on the paths was flimsy. From today's perspective it was virtually a suicide mission. The enemy were on the edge and von Senger's division suffered 50 casualties, but the enemy lost 21 tanks and 150 Russian prisoners were taken.

During 19 December and all night, the fighting continued without a pause and von Senger, who had anticipated this situation, decided to move along what he described as the north bank, but the enemy held the high ground. When the Russians had attacked Finland on 30 November 1939, many, especially the Germans thought the Red Army was weak. However, now they were under personal threat they had rapidly improved, both in officers and men, and their resources were superior with few threats to their supply lines. Such was the Russian strength that the 6th Panzer Division had to withdraw, and von Senger knew, as he anticipated that it was a defeat, even though they were only 18–19 miles from Stalingrad, and that any hope of a rescue plan was no longer possible. He knew there was no point giving a 'pep' talk to men who had been sleeping in minus 20 degrees, noting that 'any word of encouragement would have sounded hollow'. They were still holding the bridgehead but sustained more casualties, and von Senger dreaded receiving Hitler's well-known and infamous order to fight to the last man, as it would mean the destruction of his division.

It was not long before he recognised that not just his role, but the whole operation had to fail, because like Stalingrad they were in danger of being encircled. Later he reflected on Hitler's absurd demand to keep the Sixth Army in place. There were many amongst the officers who thought this was nonsensical, but the German-Prussian military sense of obedience meant Hitler was obeyed even if it meant self-destruction. At one stage in his memoirs von Senger even tried to see the importance of not accepting defeat, as such was the nature of a Russian victory it would signal the defeat of Germany. Stalin, probably like the Germans, had seen the importance of Stalingrad, not because it bore the Russian dictator's name, but it stood at a major geographical crossing point. The Russians had cleverly attacked the weaker points held by the softer German allied armies, and there was no way of turning the clock back. Had General Paulus been allowed to escape at an earlier time this may have worked, but such was the massive strength of a now well led Soviet Army even this was unlikely, and the Axis forces were now very much on the defensive. It would have made more sense had von Senger argued that some form of peace agreement may have saved the day. He concluded with the thoughtful line that the danger of staying politically passive was no answer, noting 'that it denies Clausewitz's principle of the subordination of the military to the political viewpoint'.[15]

Von Senger reflected on the battle scenes in the few days prior to 20 December, realising they had fought their way into a position and into a situation which could not be foreseen. Now it was a matter of fighting for survival. He reflected on his experience, recalling that in cavalry days the best tactical control came from the front, which was the same with the transition to armoured vehicles. In Poland, the advance had been made by tanks and the focal point of the battle tended to centre on these mobile forces. He also concluded that the artillery remained essential but had to be made as mobile as possible. However, this time in the Russian war, times had changed, because the Germans were suffering from insufficient tanks and lack of essential resources, but despite these issues the critical factor, von Senger concluded, was the mobile nature of the command. The man in charge had to see for himself what was happening and where, not from some distant safe headquarters. He also decided that the presence of the divisional commander had a 'psychological effect on the troops' which was undoubtedly true. Some of the most favoured of leading generals on a global basis have been those who have appeared on or near the front line to see for themselves what was happening, a point General Alan Brooke was always pointing out to Churchill.

Christmas Day 1942 must have been dreary for von Senger and his troops because instead of a heroic attack to relieve Stalingrad they were preparing for defence and a safe withdrawal. He noted some Romanian soldiers looked fatigued and somewhat apathetic, adding the comment 'what else could one expect?' This intimated his understanding of men caught up in a battle as virtually enforced allies of the Nazi regime. This may well have been the case with some British colonial and commonwealth troops wondering why they were fighting for their lives in some distant battle far from their natural homes. At night von Senger visited the front line and saw his troops on the vast steppes frozen and with no sensible cover with the temperature as low as minus 25 degrees. At the battle headquarters he could sense the frustration as they studied maps looking at villages which did not exist. He slept in a room with some twenty others with soldiers coming and going to keep warm and to stay alive. The suffering of the troops badly effected von Senger as he could see the extreme cold was sapping their strength, one of the few memoirs of a general to show a sense of compassion for his men. Outside were corpses which needed burying, and wounded men suffering agonies from untreated open wounds, suffering the danger of freezing to death.

Just after 1943 started, it was announced that von Senger's 17th Panzer Division would receive a new allocation of fifty tanks, and the Division was no longer alone, and although the sense of hope was not high it was rumoured that the Russians had problems with supplies, but how they could know this for a fact is somewhat dubious. There were isolated battle engagements, and von Senger had to spend more time at the Battle Headquarters, away from the focal points where the conflict was taking place. He and his adjutant found an old house in which to sleep, noting that even when facing death each day it was essential to have sleep, warmth, and some nourishment, thus underlining the basic needs for humans to stay alive, and in these wintery conditions managing to have a few hours' warmth was critical. He even had time to admire an old icon on the wall whose gold parts shone with the glimmer of a nearby candle, stirring his spirituality.

It was not long before the enemy started to push forward with a sense of unleashed power, putting the hope that the Russians were short of supplies into the nonsense box. Von Senger came to the relief of his troops by throwing more tanks in, and some of the circling formidable Russian T-34 tanks were driven out of sight. There were even plans for a German attack on various pressure points, but by 5 January the battle group started to move out of the bridgehead, but the enemy reacted quickly obviously confident of their greater strength and knowledgeable about German intentions. However, the German counter thrusts appeared to have brought some relief, and it was able to withdraw to a new defensive in some order.

The use of tanks had led to lengthy discussions by military experts across all countries which used them as weapons. Von Senger arrived at the conclusion that 'it was only through concentrating all available tanks at a single point that a worthwhile result could be achieved, albeit of short duration'.[16] Many experts might have agreed with von Senger, but not all, though it probably made sense in the circumstances which he was watching. There is no question that the Tiger tanks greatly aided the armoured troops. Von Senger was critical that the Russians did not push on with their pursuit as that was what he described a 'rule of war', but it must have been clear by now that the Russians knew what they were doing and had the upper hand. He and his men were probably also lucky that this so-called 'rule of war' was not pursued. Von Senger even wondered or hoped the enemy was running short of fuel, which was more of a German problem. On the more realistic side, von Senger noted the political strategy was wrong, as while there was some opportunity, they should have looked to end the war when the opportunity was still possible, if only for the sake of people's lives.

Interestingly, von Senger related a moment when a young local teenager (a Kalmuk youth about 16-years-old) arrived on his pony and jumped into von Senger's trench for safety from the battle. He was shaken by the battle and burst into tears. In some areas of the combat under some other commanders this may have been seen as a potentially dangerous incursion by the surprise visitor, and dealt with by a pistol shot, but von Senger's reaction was simply to note that 'I was moved by the innocence of the lad'.[17] Not long after this von Senger was woken from his sleep to receive a Hitler order which stated he would protect every officer who in the fight against partisans who did not scruple to kill women and children. Probably bearing in mind the terrified teenager, von Senger decided not to circulate the order, the first of many he would not obey. Von Senger's hope was that he would never be called upon to support such excesses, even against the dreaded partisan. This incident and Hitler's order caused him to think of his son who was fighting somewhere else on the Eastern Front. He later discovered his son had been due to fly back into the cauldron (the term used to describe Stalingrad) but fortunately he missed the flight because he had been receiving treatment in the Göttingen hospital. It was not until 23 January 1943 he heard the good news that his son had not been in Stalingrad when it was taken by the Russians, because had he survived, he would not have seen him until the early 1950s.

From 8 January it was eventually decided to find the times and the means 'to pull back' (an expression more favourable than retreat) the army of the Caucasus, which meant a vast area which the German army was too small to cover adequately. They knew that if they attacked, the Russians would respond at once with whole battalions producing the danger of being outflanked. The defence had to be mobile simply because they did not have the same resources as the Soviet Red Army, and were not helped by the tracked vehicles being seriously hindered by the frozen ground. It must have been depressing for the German troops facing a major defeat, suffering from the unbelievable cold, and wondering if they had any chance of survival, being threatened by a superior army and a winter making outdoor life virtually unsustainable. Von Senger was aware of these circumstances, and as he had made a point of being seen at the front, he was also making sure he was with them whenever a situation was becoming critical. Yet he was humble enough to admit 'I was only too conscious of the paucity of my contribution'. He admitted he had to make a personal determined effort to stand with his men rather than return to the safer divisional battle headquarters. He was right when he wrote that 'a commander who scurries away from the front line whenever there is danger soon loses the confidence of his troops'.[18] It was known from the front trenches in the First World War the attitude of the soldiers towards officers who disappeared when there were signs of an attack. Von

Senger noted that there was a relationship between the soldier and the officer who shared the danger which was 'more eloquent than any words'. He also noted with a degree of pleasure those Romanian soldiers who had stayed and had attached themselves to German units, and also the Russian Cossacks who helped because of their distrust of Stalin.

Finally, they were able to cross the Don River, and he promulgated an order to all his men which was really a note of congratulations for their fighting: 'achieving more than can be humanly expected in your uninterrupted day and night fighting for weeks on end, often while threatened from the rear and at the same time exposed to frontal attacks by armour' and he remembered the dead.[19] It was a sensitive effort to acknowledge their perseverance and courage, and a written note was probably the best and only way to accomplish this message.

Stalingrad had fallen, and von Senger commented on the problems the Sixth Army had suffered from lack of supplies. Göring had promised the Luftwaffe would drop all that was necessary, and von Senger described this as Utopian. This was almost overly sensitive, because Göring, who was hunting hares as the tragedy unfolded was known for making promises he could never keep. He did not discuss the problems with his senior Luftwaffe officers, or investigate the issues of planes available, or the dangerous airstrip, instead in his usual egotistical fashion had made a promise which could never be fulfilled. It was known by many at the time that Göring had let the Sixth Army down, and von Senger by calling it 'Utopian' was almost polite.

The day he heard his son was not in Stalingrad (23 January 1943) he received more orders to move on to Stalino (today Donetsk) making him sad at leaving the countryside, but he was encouraged by the news that he might meet his son who was now adjutant to the commander of a unit in that area. They eventually met and embraced, he had an evening meal with him, stayed in his quarters, shared breakfast, and then suffered one another's departure.

Von Senger and his division were put under the command of the 1st Panzer Army, and for most of early February his division marched rather than fought, but soon found themselves in battle in freezing weather, which von Senger noted had a strange way of absorbing the noise of battle. They had to fight their way through villages led by a few tanks, and von

Senger described how he saw the bodies of dead Russians outside the houses, describing in detail the nature of the appalling wounds which were grotesque. It had been a matter of clearing house by house, and it must have been the case that many of these were civilians hoping the war would pass them by. Von Senger tried various tactics to break through, even going with a Motor-Cycle Battalion to supervise its attack. It was often a case of being pursued, but occasionally the situation reversed as are the fortunes and mishaps on all battlefields. By 27 February as they were closing in on the Donetz (Donets) they started to find little to no opposition. Von Senger described how they passed through another battle scene again describing the terrible things he saw which almost defy the imagination. His descriptions of the realities tend to reflect his personal horror.

The general thrust of war in this area was a series of local battles trying to establish or attack various bridgeheads, with von Senger noting how resolute the Russians proved to be in defence. By early summer von Senger's war on the Eastern Front finished when he was summoned during June 1943 to Hitler's headquarters, the Obersalzberg (often known as the Berghof, the Eagle's Nest) during one of Hitler's daily conferences.

Chapter 3

War In Three Mediterranean Islands

The Battle for Sicily

Von Senger felt that Hitler's assignment and instructions for sending him to the Mediterranean were not exactly clear, as he had been told he was responsible for the defence of Sicily, but only in the capacity as the liaison officer to the Italian 6th Army Command under Guzzoni. He was, however, 'provided with a small operation and a signals company so that he could exercise emergency control'.[1]

The Allies had considered invading Sardinia, but the British had persuaded their American Allies that Sicily could have aircover and was closer to the Italian mainland. After Operation *Torch* the Germans had realised an incursion into southern Europe was likely. To mislead the Axis as to the precise target-areas various ruses were offered to enemy observers with Anglo-American ships sailing towards Norway, others towards Greece and the Balkans. Perhaps the most famous deception was Operation *Mincemeat* when the British left a corpse, supposedly a British officer, on a Spanish beach with a briefcase full of plans for the Balkan area. As anticipated the Spanish shared the information with the Germans and many but not all were fooled. Some thought Sardinia and many believed the Balkans to be the target, not least because Churchill's penchant for that 'soft underbelly' was well known. Mussolini and Kesselring, the German Commander-Chief-South were not fooled, and they still retained spies in North Africa. According to von Senger, Hitler was concerned whether the two German divisions already on Sicily were sufficient for defence without calling on Italian troops. Hitler was concerned about the political weaknesses in Italy and whether it would defect, and there was a sense of general unease about the Italian forces, looking at von Senger with what he described as a 'mistrustful eye', telling him that of course von Senger knew Italy well. Von Senger added the line that the so-called hold Hitler had over people made no impression on him, but earlier he had noted Hitler's excellent brain for remembering detail. It is true that according to many accounts Hitler seemed to have a magnetic effect on even senior commanders, probably based on his own form of charisma and his military success in France, where he had been proved correct; some used to call it the 'command bug'.

There were, von Senger discovered, some who were less certain about the viability of defending Sicily. He had lunch with General Warlimont who thought if the Allies launched an attack on Sicily, it was probably best to transfer the troops to the mainland. He also claimed Keitel expressed the same sentiments, which would have been unusual as Keitel was known for always supporting Hitler whether right or wrong.

Officially, the Italian General Alfredo Guzzoni was expected to command the Axis forces, but having arrived in Sicily in May, he found it badly defended. He was told there was no substantial air force, that the ground troops were untrained, but like Mussolini he had been convinced Sicily was the next target. One historian noted that Guzzoni had 'to alter the deeply rooted inferiority complex that had pervaded the Italian army since the beginning of the war', but another consideration was that many Italians did not want to engage in war with the Western powers.[2] At this stage the Germans were being cautious, as von Senger was a mere liaison officer purportedly to defend Sicily, and his immediate boss, Field Marshal Kesselring, also had to adhere, seemingly, to the demands of the Italian *Comando Supremo* (Italian High Command). Hitler had long admired Mussolini, but he was politically astute enough to have doubts about his strength as a dictator and military tactician.

Kesselring had been given to understand that he was to be in charge of all matters military in Italy, but subject to the 'complex Italian command and the OKW and Hitler'.[3] It was a strange appointment in so far that Hitler wanted to impose his military authority through Kesselring, but the Italians were bemused, viewing Kesselring as a senior liaison officer who would, within a short space of time, be known by the Allies under the code name of 'the Emperor', such was the nature of control which he eventually attained in Italy.[4]

A few days later von Senger met Kesselring in Rome but in a vastly different atmosphere from that of Obersalzberg. Kesselring was known by the Allies as Smiling Albert because he always appeared pleasant and happy with life.* Generally, many colleagues liked him, with the exception of Rommel, and he was always optimistic. This latter aspect of his character disturbed von Senger for a time because Kesselring was convinced that Sicily could resist any invasion, but von Senger was less certain. Kesselring believed it possible to resist any invasion from the sea by hitting them as they landed. Von Senger even mentioned the clash with Rommel, which was to develop later as Rommel, now out of North Africa, was keen to take charge in Italy. However, he found that Kesselring's attitude towards the Italians was more gentlemanly and less critical than that of Rommel, which von Senger felt to be right. It was not so much a moral consideration but political, because it would be a tricky situation when fighting the Allies if they also had the Italians turn against them, but Kesselring accepted the German primacy in military conduct on their own territory. Kesselring's views of the Italians were typical of his background in which professional militarism was given undue priority. Unlike Rommel he was more able to conceal his contempt for Italian command, but both of them only observed the situation militarily, and misunderstood the Italian people. His subordinate, the more perceptive von Senger, was probably closer to the truth when he wrote that 'the Italian is by nature more critical and therefore politically more mature than the Germans', and they had quickly realised they were in a hopeless situation.[5]

During most of the campaign in Italy there was an ongoing conflict as to which German Field Marshal was in charge, Rommel or Kesselring, and even Hitler at times appeared uncertain. Eventually Rommel's prestigious status started to fade despite Goebbel's propaganda, and Hitler moved more towards the optimistic Kesselring whose strategy was one of defence up the leg of Italy which Hitler found more appealing. Von Senger would later find that many officers still hero-worshipped Rommel.

Later, when von Senger met Field Marshal von Richthofen in charge of Air Fleet 2, the meeting was less amicable because von Senger discovered Richthofen had moved his main Luftwaffe defences to Sardinia, convinced like many others that this was the likely target for an invasion. Von

* Kesselring was a Luftwaffe Field Marshal, but in Italy would oversee the army and at times the German Navy (Kriegsmarine) which was the first time such power existed.

Senger found it regrettable that these two German Field Marshals held different viewpoints.

On 26 June von Senger had a meeting with Kesselring and Guzzoni to discuss how they would prepare in the event of Sicily being invaded. Von Senger had already noted that the coastal Italian divisions were not the best as they were immobile and inadequately armed. In the eastern part of Sicily was the German 15th Panzer Grenadier Division and a second, the Hermann Göring Division was on its way. There were other dispersed Italian divisions and again not the best equipped. Officially, the Italian General Alfredo Guzzoni was supposed to oversee the Axis forces, having arrived in Sicily in May when he found it poorly defended. He discovered there was next to no air force and the ground troops hardly trained, and like Field Marshal Albert Kesselring, he had been convinced Sicily was the next target. Guzzoni had 'to alter the deeply rooted inferiority complex that had pervaded the Italian army since the beginning of the war'.[6]

In Rome, the Italians had informed Kesselring that Sicily's defences were satisfactory, but after flying there he formed a different view. He discovered gun-emplacement constructions which were mere 'eyewash' and altogether the defences 'all so much gingerbread'.[7] The Todt organisation used reinforced concrete, but many of the Italian constructions, viewable today, show gun-emplacements made from brick covered with thin cement.* Kesselring flew in construction teams to work with Italian labour, but time was against them. Von Senger watched these preparations taking place, but also noted the continuous debates about where they should be situated. The Italians wanted the gun emplacements out of sight of naval guns, the German wanted them closer to the beach to create havoc as landing craft approached. Another issue that von Senger picked up was that although the island had plenty of necessary stores, they were all situated on the west side. They were also having immense difficulties with communications, which meant von Senger had no immediate links with Kesselring, and even at the Italian 6th Army Headquarters there was no radio or landline communications with Rome. With all the military

* The writer saw such defences in 2012: red brick and thin concrete looking like 'gingerbread'.

units spread around the island and many with next to no mobility it was far from reassuring.

Von Senger observed on 26 June that in a meeting at Enna (centre of the island perched on a mountain) Kesselring offered good advice, and he was always polite and tactful with Guzzoni. However, there was a significant gap between the two as Kesselring was convinced of victory should they invade, whereas Guzzoni was only too happy to express his more sceptical outlook. However, Guzzoni had seen the German forces fighting in North Africa and accepted Kesselring's assurance, and also wanted to avoid any enmity between the two national militaries. Although Kesselring was diplomatic and careful with the Italians there was a deep suspicion over the presence of such a senior German military figure. Mussolini's son-in-law Ciano wrote in his diary regarding Kesselring that 'Mussolini has swallowed a toad', suggesting he had swallowed poison or something that would consume him in turn.[8]

The German contingent in trying to keep Guzzoni and the Italians comfortable in their company accepted many of the plans over which the Germans had doubts, not least the necessity of hitting the Allies as they landed, and Guzzoni's idea that the two stronger German units should be kept further inland, where not only would they be exposed to air attacks but would be facing landed troops rather than when they were finding their land-feet. Kesselring argued and won the debate that the two German divisions should not be stationed together, but one in the east and the other in the west.

As von Senger unfolded the drama of the invasion, either for reasons of politeness or for the sake of postwar German-Italian relationships, he made no major reference to the fact that the Italians on the coastal line and elsewhere surrendered in droves. It was a form of self-demobilisation, as many Italians had ceased to be enamoured with Mussolini's fascist regime, and many had not wanted the war in the first place. There is no doubt that many had family relations living in America and Britain. They had been disillusioned by their German partners who had often scorned them as lacking military prowess, and have since attracted the criticism of being cowards, which is a total falsehood. The same had happened in North Africa and Italian soldiery attracted tasteless humour. The war photographer Robert Capa wrote about the Sicilian invasion stating that it 'turned out to be a twenty-one-day race and in the lead was the Italian Army. They were afraid not only of the Americans, but of the Germans too, and ran in every direction'.[9] General Omar Bradley observed 'that the Italian coastal troops stampeded to the safety of our prisoner of war cages on the beach in such terrific disorder that our troops faced greater danger from being trampled upon than from bullets'.[10] Overall nearly 9,000 Italians welcomed the opportunity of becoming prisoners of war, creating for Bradley's II Corps the pressing problem of Italian prisoners who had to be contained, fed and watered. There were 'more enemy soldiers captured in a week than were bagged by the U.S. Army in all of World War I'.[11] They were not cowards, but they had grown tired of fascism and its promises and wanted a return to normality. Von Senger was later in his work to note that the Italians, on the whole, were politically more astute than their German counterparts many of whom accepted Hitler's regime to the end.[12]

When the Italians showed signs of collapsing, the Chief-of-Army Staff, General Roatta, suggested to General Ambrosio the need to reinforce the air units in the area which only the Germans could do. Ambrosio submitted the matter to Kesselring, with Mussolini writing a letter to Hitler about the necessity of more German air units to defend Sicily. This was the only way to prevent the fall of Sicily, with all the moral and military repercussions.[13]

Meanwhile, von Senger was critical of the Hermann Göring Division stationed in the east because it had some notable weaknesses as it was on the weakside. According to von Senger 'in personnel the Hermann Göring Division had certain defects, but at that time the higher authorities were unaware of this'.[14] Von Senger even pointed out that two of its leading officers were unfit to lead in action, though he offered no details to why. He even wondered if Kesselring, as a Luftwaffe officer, had some pressure applied on him by his immediate superior Göring.

On 9 July von Senger heard from spotter plane pilots that convoys were heading for the island and at 05.00 the next morning reports were received of enemy parachutists. What von Senger would not have known was that many of the Allied parachute drops were disasters as many of the planes flew at night, some for the first time in the dark, many were dropped in the wrong places, and some lost at sea. This parachute attack was coded

Operation *White Pyjamas* a night-drop with 2,300 men expected to jump from 144 planes before midnight. Many experienced officers suggested it should be done in daylight, but General George Patton ignored the warnings and simply instructed the home fleet not to fire at aircraft. One nervous gunner had not heard the command or thought he knew better firing his gun, which was instantly followed by hundreds of others. Von Senger was aware that these troops also suffered considerable losses from the German AA batteries, and later paratroopers were fired on by their own side. On 11 July, the Axis had launched nearly 500 aerial attacks, most of them in the American area and this no doubt had increased the sense of nervousness, as Patton noted later 'men who have been bombed all day get itchy fingers'.[15] There were considerable tensions within the German-Italian areas of command, with Kesselring in Rome often objecting to decisions made by Guzzoni even when supported by von Senger. Kesselring's main concern was overthrowing the Allies at Gela as they landed, which with the benefit of hindsight was probably the better judgement. Many of the coastal areas were within Italian hands, and as noted above, their hearts were not in the fight, and there were no incidents of serious Italian counter offences. Guzzoni, like General Warlimont earlier had no conviction in the Axis ability to be able to defend Sicily.

On 12 July Kesselring arrived at the Enna headquarters to talk with von Senger and Guzzoni about what was happening. It transpired, according to von Senger, that Kesselring was being given misleading information by the 2nd Fliegerkorps stationed in Sicily, ranging from the 'over optimistic while others were alarmist'. Kesselring was pondering the possibility of sending more troops over from the mainland, which immediately clashed with Guzzoni and von Senger, who were thinking of delaying action to allow evacuation, resulting in the command sent out from headquarters. However, on the same day some reinforcements crossed over. The very next day Guzzoni's headquarters in Enna were hit by an Allied bombing raid, and von Senger had to convince Guzzoni to move out as he wished to stay with his men. Von Senger had been anticipating an Allied invasion of the west coast, but now realised this was not going to happen, but was still concerned there might be another incursion in the northern area. It was at this stage that some problems emerged with the Hermann Göring Division, most notably their slowness, causing von Senger to suspect that Göring might be interfering from the relative safety of Germany. It was the night-dropping parachutists which unnerved Guzzoni, and he had wanted the Hermann Göring Division to counterattack but they claimed they were too busy elsewhere, even though it was known that they were not under heavy pressure. Again, von Senger tended to blame Kesselring because he was Luftwaffe and had to listen to Göring. However, von Senger acknowledged that Kesselring was having to deal with the OKW while accepting the authority of the Italian command. Von Senger was also worried because it was slowly dawning on him that the Italians might give up the fight which would mean the Germans would be fighting with no help. Kesselring, who may have felt the same, even started to short-circuit his messages to von Senger and other German commanders keeping the Italians in the dark. It was clear that the OKW were insisting, as usual, that it was a matter of standing firm. As soon as the scale of the Allied invasion became crystal clear, especially in the south, 'Guzzoni and von Senger had not hesitated to recall the 15th Panzer Grenadier Division from Western Sicily' as soon as it was apparent the direction the Allies were taking.[16]

On 16 July Kesselring suddenly ordered that General Hans Hube would be taking charge of all German troops in Sicily, which came as a surprise to von Senger who was, by this command, reminded he was only the liaison officer for the Italians. None of this was helped when German reinforcements arrived without motors, so they took the Italian vehicles who were seemingly not fighting, which led to some fatalities on both sides. A deepening fissure was opening between the two Axis powers. General Hube suggested to Guzzoni that the Italian 6th Army should be moved to Calabria (region in southern Italy around the 'toe') which Guzzoni rightly informed him was a decision which had to be made by the Commando Supremo.

Von Senger took time after outlining the Axis defence system to reflect on the lessons from the failure, focusing on the problems when dealing with an invasion force landing by sea from a superior naval power backed by aircraft. He identified as a weakness the German traditions which were mainly based on land warfare. He knew that during the interbellum years, while he was enjoying the cavalry and the company of his beloved horses, that von Seeckt, assisted by others including Kesselring, had formulated the tactic of airpower and land forces working together. He was correct however, that the German military had neglected the impact of a powerful navy assisting a coastal invasion. Germany although a huge country had more land than sea borders, unlike Britain defined by a totally encompassing coastline and a coastal invasion would not have seemed necessary for such planning. Germany, having expanded its borders under Hitler, was now discovering the need for more advanced tactical and strategic studies in this hitherto ignored area.

It had been claimed that some captured Italian generals had told Eisenhower that the landings were a total surprise. Von Senger rebuffed this in his memoirs, but he admitted that while they knew an invasion fleet was underway, they remained not only uncertain as to whether it would be Sicily or Sardinia, but where and in how many places the landings would take place on an exceptionally long coastline being an island. Nor had consideration been given to the power and precise aiming ability of naval guns. On land it was virtually impossible to find safety from naval guns which always appeared too accurate. As von Senger had noted, the Italians wanted their defence out of sight of naval guns, but Kesselring wanted them close to the beaches, and 'the resulting controversy was still raging when the invasion commenced'.[17] Kesselring later admitted his surprise at the accuracy of the naval guns and admitted they had made a powerful impression upon him.[18] The same naval guns could also be used against land troops deep in land with their formidable range. Von Senger also added the fact that recent developments meant that tanks could be landed at the same time as troops, though as the Dieppe landing effort had demonstrated, they needed the right sort of beach surface to be useful.

Von Senger also challenged later accounts of the Sicilian invasion when some claimed the Allied success was down to official Italian treachery and command difficulties in the Axis command. The Allied success he attributed to sea power and superior resources, not helped by Sicily's long coastline having few fortifications. He was right that it was unlikely that there had been official treachery, but even he had to admit in his memoirs that Kesselring and other senior Germans had found relationships with the Italians difficult at times. Nor did he reflect on the fact that many Italian soldiers had surrendered because, as mentioned above, they had no feelings of loyalty towards Hitler or even Mussolini.

Because von Senger was much more of an intellectual than most of his contemporaries, and although he goes into detail about the various battlelines, he spends time on the wider front of politics, relationships, and adds a postwar commentary on the ramifications of what he witnessed. He was, for example, defensive of the Italians whereas the German military was becoming more derisory of their forces, and they were mocked by many of the Allies. He refused to accept that they were treacherous, and pointed out that their attitudes changed as they realised that their alliance with Nazi Germany was turning the future against them. Von Senger realised that it was important to keep Italy onside, and as such it was essential that their military was not humiliated. He believed it critical that the Italians should not be given the impression that the war was exclusively of German interest, or that they were puppets instructed to do what and when. Field Marshal Rommel had made it clear that the North African war had become a German war, and he and many other German military were derisory about their Italian counterparts, with jokes about Italian soldiers being widespread. Von Senger pointed out that even when it was announced Mussolini had fallen from power the Italian 6th Army had remained loyal to the Germans, which von Senger used to stop the later German puppet government executing Guzzoni.

Von Senger also claimed that like many other officers he felt the war was lost. To those not inclined to see Hitler as a military deity and who had some understanding of warfare this was undoubtedly true. The loss of Stalingrad and its Sixth Army had seen the northern European theatre of war, which was the most critical, turn the tide against Nazi Germany. The loss of North Africa with as many if not more German PoWs than Stalingrad was followed by invading southern Europe, which for Nazi Germany was another danger signal. In addition to these signs of impending failure, the North Atlantic U-boat war was turning against the Kriegsmarine, and the bombing over Germany by America in the day and the British by night was devastating. Being militarily astute and not fixated on Hitler's self-assurance and Goebbels' propaganda, it could be assumed that the intelligent von Senger held this view as he prepared to leave Sicily.

Von Senger observed that when the time came to evacuate Axis troops to the mainland, many German commanders asked to keep their Italian units to act in defence to enable the transit of troops across the Medina Straits. This task of defence fell to two German and four Italian divisions. Von Senger prepared to cross the straits after he had handed command over, but often found himself hiding in the woods from the constant air-attacks. He and Guzzoni ate together in the Italian's war caravan enjoying their food while wondering about the future. It dawned on von Senger that for the Italians, once they lost Libya, it felt as if they had lost the war, and now Sicily was being occupied their homeland was being seriously threatened. Guzzoni had accepted the new Italian government headed by Badoglio, that the war should continue, but in the confidence of the meal conversations Guzzoni suggested the Italian King (Victor Emmanuel III) would have no intention of following the road to national destruction, and he believed the king knew the war was finished.

As is now well-known Badoglio also intended ending the war as he also foresaw that it had become a lost cause. It was confusing for both von Senger and Guzzoni who had trusted one another enough to admit that neither of them was enthusiastic about their respective political regimes. Eventually General Ernst-Günther Baade, whom von Senger had helped with the evacuation of Sicily had crossed the straits to take von Senger over to the mainland. His main job as liaison officer with the Italian 6th Army was now done.

From the German point of view, it may have appeared as a failure, but the fact that many Germans and some Italian troops were able to retreat to the mainland could almost be regarded as a victory in defeat, in the same way that Dunkirk had been viewed. When Kesselring had recognised that Sicily would be lost, he had promptly ordered the evacuation. Baade had quickly made Messina the most heavily defended spot in Europe, and eventually 12,000 German troops and 4,000 vehicles were evacuated to the mainland, with the forecast there was time for those fighting to be evacuated in five nights. This was a major and life-saving effort by the Germans who were surprised that the Allies did not attack the crossing using their air superiority. British eavesdroppers had listened in and picked up what the Germans were doing, and Alexander had been warned the week before, but no plans had been made about thwarting the Messina Strait escape, or even one swiftly improvised, despite the obvious urgency of trapping the Germans. Baade's guns could point upwards, and the new

German 88mm Flak 81 could reach 25,000 feet against bombers, and Air Command was reluctant to risk their best B-17s. The Naval Command was equally unprepared to let their big ships enter a narrow space with limited manoeuvrability. The Germans found themselves unmolested and started evacuating in daylight. At Dunkirk, the British out of sheer determination had evacuated the BEF and many French, but they left their weapons and machines whereas in Sicily the Germans managed to extricate their entire force with their essential weaponry. The campaign had pushed the Germans out of Sicily but not trapped or destroyed them.

British Lieutenant Colonel Lionel Wigram recognised this in his unfavourable report which concluded that 'the Germans have undoubtedly in one way scored a decided success in Sicily' and was promptly sacked by Montgomery.[19] Although defeated by retreating from Sicily and the German-Italian command structure was criticised for its 'fractured approach', the Allied command was at times just as brittle in its command structure. Montgomery had demanded that the American General Omar Bradley stand aside to allow his own troops passage, and for some critics all this did was slow possible progress. General Patton suddenly swung west to take Palermo, criticised by many, others believed it essential, and one of Field Marshal Alexander's (the man responsible for the invasion plans) biographers wrote that it 'was a necessary part of the campaign, to provide Patton with a port instead of the open beaches to which Montgomery's plan had restricted him. Yet even ignoring the fact that Patton was being supplied through Syracuse and Augusta, to say nothing of the recent American capture of Porto Empedolce, Palermo was useless as a port since the enemy had most effectively blocked its harbour by sinking some forty ships in it'.[20]

Von Senger may have noted that if there had been tensions between the Germans and the Italians there was friction between the Americans and British. The Western Allies by not foreseeing the possible retreat of Axis troops across the Messina Straits missed the opportunity of trapping valuable German Divisions and those Italians still willing to fight; such is the nature of war and the flaws of command.

From Sicily to Corsica and Sardinia

On the mainland von Senger drove up the west coast and had to dive for cover when enemy bombers appeared overhead. He found Naples in a bad way with evident hunger and sickness prevalent amongst the residents he observed. They spent the second night in Cassino town, and at the top of the overlooking mountain they visited the world-famous Monte Cassino Abbey, a Benedictine foundation (built around 529) where Saint Benedict of Nursia had once composed the well-known Rule of St Benedict. This meant a great deal to von Senger as an ardent Roman Catholic and Lay Benedictine, often known as a Benedictine Oblate, who follow the Benedictine rules but do not live in a religious community, and who adhere (or try) to the rule of St Benedict. He had lunch with the Abbot, Gregorio IV Diamare, and discovered General Hans Hube had close contact with the monastery. What von Senger did not realise at this time was that soon he would be back in the Abbey at one of the most critical times in its existence.

Away from the spirituality of the Abbey he reported to Kesselring on 11 August and was pleased to find his 'boss' was in a pleasant mood. Von Senger does not write much on the matter, but it was highly likely that Kesselring had gathered from von Senger's reactions and views while in Sicily, a man with sound tactical and strategic viewpoints from an officer he would have considered as a mere minor general. Not least, most of von Senger's predictions and warnings had been proved right. Kesselring even gave him a photograph of himself with a flattering inscription. Von Senger was often critical of Kesselring's well-known optimism, did not always agree with his decisions, but the critical and deeply religious von Senger, who opposed the NSDAP, wrote that he admired Kesselring, whom he also recognised as a person torn between duty to his country and the evil of their political masters. This was a common attitude postwar, but given Kesselring's character, probably not an unreasonable assumption that he felt this at the time.

He was with Kesselring when he held an interview with the newly appointed Minster of Marine (Navy), but von Senger found it difficult to work out what line the new man was taking. It was eventually agreed that the Italian Fleet would stay in its harbours of La Spezia and Taranto.

The general feeling seemed to be that if they put to sea then they would become the object of direct attack by superior Royal Navy ships and aircraft. The British would not wait for them to leave harbour as they had proved in November 1940 by aircraft attack, which was so successful it has been claimed the Japanese formulated the idea for Pearl Harbor. Another factor not raised in the meeting was that by 1943 the Italians had next to no fuel supplies to allow major ships out of their harbours.

Kesselring provided von Senger with a plane and within two hours he landed at Munich and caught a train to his hometown of Göttingen. It was not long before he was given a new assignment, one he did not relish as it amounted to a stark reminder of Sicily. He was to be the commander of the Wehrmacht forces to take charge of the German evacuation of Sardinia and the defence of Corsica. He was aware of the strain between the German high command and the Badoglio government and wondered how far there would be cooperation. He was sure the Badoglio government would 'leave them to their own devices' which was hardly an attractive situation. Kesselring had already warned him that if this transpired to be the case the Italians had to be disarmed, but numerically on the island the Germans were greatly outnumbered.

Once Italian, Corsica had long been French and had come under the administration of Vichy France, but after the Allied success in North Africa in November 1942, Hitler took over the whole of France, and German and Italian troops had occupied the island. For some Italians it was seen as an act of irredentism, the recovery of their own land, but as Ciano had noted Corsica and its people felt they were French and saw the Italians as hostile occupiers. It was not long before there was a form of French Resistance whom von Senger referred to as 'insurgents'. It has been estimated that in Corsica there were 80,000 plus Italian troops and about 12,000 Germans, while the civilian population was approximately 220,000, making 2–3 civilians for every occupying foreign soldier.

On 7 September 1943, von Senger flew into Ajaccio, his staff arriving from Leghorn (Livorno) on the Tuscany coast opposite Corsica. Four days earlier on 3 September Italy had surrendered and signed an armistice, which became public on 8 September. Reading von Senger's own notes it seems that he either knew of this or that it was highly likely and anticipated any moment, but he had arrived just as the pot was reaching boiling point. When von Senger called on the Italian commander, General Magli, he gathered he was pro-German and had been told by Kesselring that he could be trusted, though he wrote 'yet I noticed a very frigid atmosphere among the officers'.[21] Von Senger was also aware that if the Italians 'changed sides' they had to be disarmed, it was called Operation *Achse*, originally called *Alaric*. In Sicily as in Sardinia there were many more Italian than German soldiers creating a delicate situation for von Senger. When following Kesselring's instructions, he asked that German units should assist on the coastal batteries, but Magli refused as he had already done with Kesselring. The only strong point von Senger had was that the SS-Assault Brigade Reichsführer SS was well equipped, and at that time was alert to any enemy landings and looking after the southern port of Bonfacio in the event of taking in German troops from

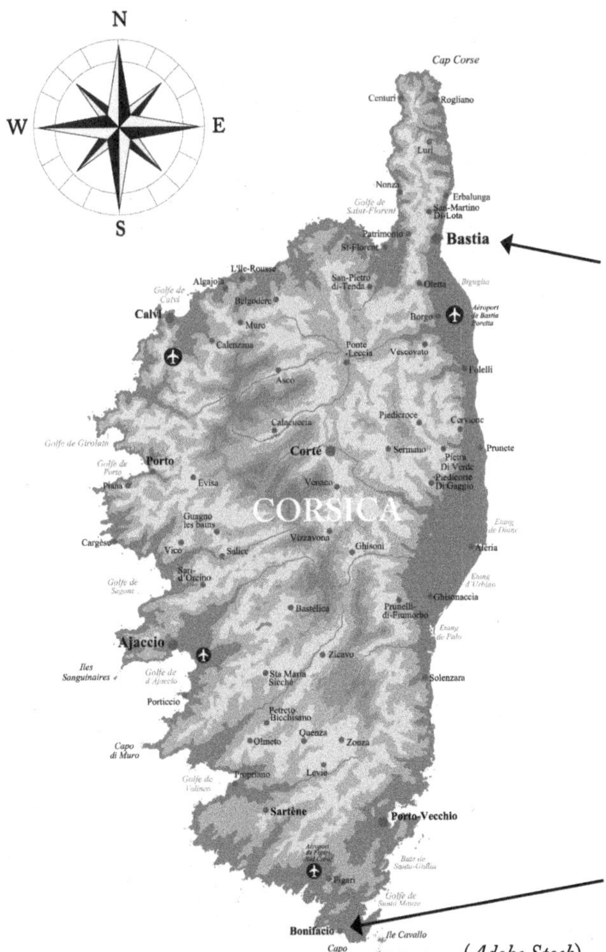

The main points of concern

The port of Bastia opposite mainland Italy

Bonifacio close for Sardinia evacuation

(*Adobe Stock*)

Sardinia. Von Senger found himself allocated to the Italian VII Army Corps commanders in the same position he had been in Sicily. Von Senger was aware that the Italian forces were watching the west coast, but the east coast was vulnerable especially the harbour of Bastia in the north, so von Senger decided to spread his men along the east coast and Magli approved this decision.

As soon as Eisenhower had signed the Armistice (4 September 1943) the Italian War Office prepared *Memorandum OP 44* to face and presumably fight the Germans, but it was only known to a small clique at the War Office. When the news came through in Corsica, a Colonel Massa who had heard it on a London broadcast, went to inform General Magli who was dining with von Senger. 'The meal ended less warmly than it had begun. Magli told Senger that in accordance with Badoglio's broadcast the Italians would not resist Anglo-American landings but knowing nothing of *Memorandum OP 44* he said the Germans were free to leave the island'.[22]

The next day, as noted above, the situation for von Senger changed radically. The Badoglio government had agreed that all Italian forces were to be neutralised which prompted the French resistance to act, as General Magli had no serious command. He promised von Senger to help against the French resistance and to assist in the evacuation of German troops from Sardinia. Using the code-word *Axis* von Senger moved the SS-Brigade into Bonifacio to ensure the arriving troops from Sardinia faced no problems. Without von Senger's knowledge the German naval garrison in Bastia made a raid on the harboured Italian naval ships, but they failed as they were resisted by the Italians who were vastly superior in numbers, meaning there were casualties both sides. All this was done without von Senger's knowledge, and he had to placate the Italian commander-in-chief, knowing he had to wait for more troops from Sardinia before he could be more pro-active. In the port of Bastia twenty-five Italian troops were killed, and 'after the battle Senger went to Magli's Headquarters and expressed sorrow about the Bastia fighting. Magli then agreed that the Germans could use the east coast of Corsica for embarkation and emphasised that he would not tolerate any further acts of hostility'.[23]

Von Senger started to head towards Bastia for the discussions on this issue but failed to reach the meeting as he came under fire from the French resistance, who were taking appropriate advantage of the situation between the one-time Axis partners. However, the 90 Panzer Grenadier Division had reached Bonifacio by 12 September, but he also heard that on the mainland German troops had already started to disarm the Italian soldiers, and the order of no further cooperation with their one-time allies even as neutrals. General Magli was evidently aware of the developing situation and surprised von Senger by agreeing that German soldiers could now help man the coastal defences, while he concentrated his troops more centrally against possible French insurrection, but he insisted on staying in Bastia because of its connection with the mainland. Unlike Sardinia the Italians in Corsica were like the Germans, occupiers of part of French territory, and the Italians refused to be disarmed. Von Senger sympathised with this as they could not disarm and then face the French insurgents. Von Senger, however, took the precaution of moving his headquarters away because he realised with the number of deficiencies, he could easily be taken prisoner by the Italians, and the time would soon arise when the German troops would have to secure Bastia by force of arms as their escape route to the mainland.

It was a stroke of good fortune that the German Sardinia commander General Carl-Hans Lungershausen had excellent personal relationships with the Italian commander-in-chief. This enabled the Germans to retain their weapons while leaving Sardinia for Corsica. The Italian commander was a General Basso who was indicted for cooperating with the Germans, but after nearly two years in prison was acquitted. As is often the case the top men took the credit for the success of the island-hopping escape by the Germans, first Kesselring, then some pointed to the work of von Senger, but it was Lungershausen and Basso's civilised relationship based on being one-time comrades until politicians decided otherwise, which saved the day. Von Senger at least acknowledged Lungershausen's achievement. There had been no attempt made to disarm one another, even though in Sardinia they had been on neutral territory. Had one side decided to disarm the other, the Italians would have probably won but it would have been a heedless bloody battle, which two civilised generals avoided.

In Corsica, the situation in Bastia was becoming both delicate and urgent, as it was the one port close enough to the mainland for the Germans to retreat towards. Von Senger had been uncertain about the quality of the German troops in Corsica when he arrived, and he was concerned that the naval garrison had failed in securing the port. He had only been there a day so had little time for a serious estimation of the situation. He was busy walking a continuous tread mill to have time for a major examination of German strength. He knew he had to convince the Italians that all the Germans required was to leave the island. The Italian local command should have realised that the Badoglio government by the armistice and surrender would not be appreciated, as they were still occupying French territory and would soon need to follow the same route back to the mainland. Von Senger had discovered that the young Luftwaffe commander was not happy about being subordinate to von Senger, but he was recalled to the mainland leaving an older and more sensible commander in place. This was critical for von Senger as he was planning a major evacuation by air. The SS unit on the island, very separate from the Wehrmacht and often despised by army officers, von Senger found to be highly cooperative. The SS tended to be and act independently, but von Senger found the senior officers of the Waffen-SS to be cooperative and willing to take instructions, writing 'that in fairness I must admit that the officers of the Waffen-SS with whom I had any dealings were always correct and modest'.[24] He also added the note that he was equally aware that the SS often reported back to their seniors on any political weaknesses they spotted amongst the commanders. This would have been a constant source of concern for von Senger whose political attitudes towards the Nazi regime often became known, and his often more civilised behaviour was noted. Later he would be recalled to Berlin for what amounted to a political correction course.

The Italians, undoubtedly concerned about reaction from the mainland continued to refuse access to Bastia, and so the German troops there were withdrawn as it was deemed essential by von Senger that the S.S. Brigade would have to amount an attack. Von Senger had made Kesselring aware of the situation, who in turn sent a telegram to be given to General Magli reminding him of how they had once fought together as comrades and expressing his friendship. The telegram was conveyed to Magli by an officer waving a flag of truce. Von Senger found the reply somewhat evasive and in places accusatory. As such Kesselring promptly ordered that the Italians should be disarmed. This was, for von Senger, an alarming command, as the only Italians within reach were those who von Senger cynically noted preferred to be German and not French prisoners. In the meantime, the SS Brigade had broken through and reached the south of the port, despite the Italians having managed to blow up an essential road bridge, but because a railway bridge could be used the attack was set to be continued the next day (13 September). Von Senger attended the attack and saw it was going to be slow as the Italians had arranged batteries on the hill above, and it became a duel between Italian and German gun-batteries. On the next day he returned to establish a bridgehead. The situation was not straightforward as the Italians had not only now accepted the support of some French resistance, but Free French troops had landed at Ajaccio on the west coast.

Von Senger had just reached the stage when he had control of Bastia, and the Italians had withdrawn away from the coast, when he was informed of a message conveying Hitler's instruction, that all Italian officers captured were to be shot and their names noted and passed on. Von Senger wrote that these men were only obeying the legitimate demands of their government, and many had been friends. Von Senger decided it was an order he would refuse to obey. It was evident that von Senger did not regard this instruction as legitimate and was taking a moral stand. At the Nuremberg Trials the question of obeying illegal and immoral orders was designated as criminal. He knew that refusing an order would not put him in a favourable light, but his sense of morality came first and foremost. He was grateful to Kesselring for accepting his decision, who later sent over his Chief of Staff instructing von Senger that the island was not to be defended. This made imminent sense as the forces would be needed for more vital operations than defending a small island. Von Senger had under him at these stage some 30,000 men, over 20,000 were army and the rest various strands of the Luftwaffe, and it was decided the safest way was to airlift the troops, which demanded a careful withdrawal paying attention to their flanks, with the need to evacuate 3,000 men each day.

Von Senger was astonished on 16 September when Kesselring's Chief of Staff, General Westphal brought the order to take the mountain roads and reconquer the island before leaving. Von Senger found the order simply nonsensical, as did Westphal who returned to explain the situation to Kesselring. On 19 September Kesselring flew to the island, saw for himself, and gave the go ahead for the evacuation. In a few years Kesselring would be admired for his defensive skills, and the tendency has been for most historians to portray Kesselring as a master of defence, bearing the 'stamp of genius'.[25] Allied commanders such as Bradley spoke highly of him, and especially Alexander, his opposite number.[26] As such, this extraordinary idea of recapturing the island did not sound like him, and it is tempting to speculate that he had received these absurd orders from Hitler or the OKW.

The evacuation continued with troops leaving by air and their equipment by sea, but the enemy were also becoming more active both at sea and in the air. There was also the problem that Free French troops were launching attacks from Ajaccio, supported by colonial troops and American tanks, they even came close enough to threaten von Senger's headquarters at Bastia. The Allies had already attacked Bastia with air-raids sinking a few vessels and damaging the port. Later the attacks destroyed some ferries, and the airports were also damaged. The air-transports were also seriously hit, with von Senger recording that on 25 September eleven Junker transport planes were shot down. Von Senger decided to move his headquarters to the south of the town, but he was suffering from a slight bout of malaria. The attacks on the airport were persistent and soon they were totally reliant on the sea channels.

The battle in Corsica was virtually over as von Senger was surrounded, on land by the Free French, and at sea the danger of submarines. He eventually left the harbour, which was being heavily shelled, waiting to the last moment to make sure all who could be evacuated had left. He was exhausted and fell into a deep sleep being woken when they arrived in the port of Leghorn. He was aware that his son whom he had last seen in Russia was on the Leghorn defences. They enjoyed meeting again and even spent some time in Florence, and the news headlines were full of the safe evacuation of Corsica. He saw as much of his son as he could, as the young man was about to be reallocated back to Russia.

He even received a telegram from Hitler congratulating him, but von Senger was more than aware that his refusal to obey an order would have left him on the blacklist. The telegram was justified because von Senger's organisational skills and persistence meant thousands of German troops had managed to escape the two island prisons for the critical fighting on the mainland. He managed this despite the overwhelming supremacy of the Allies naval and airpower in locking Sardinia and Corsica down as potential prisons by incarcerating much German fighting power. His achievement is often overlooked, and he does not dwell on it in his memoirs, but the potential loss of so many German troops would have been a major setback.

On 11 October he spent a few days at Kesselring's headquarters catching up on the mainland battles. Kesselring had hoped the Allies would land on the mainland where they had sufficient troops to stop them being successful. Von Senger noted that this wish had not been successful, Montogomery had landed safely on the Calabrian toe (Operation *Baytown*) and a landing had taken place at Salerno (Operation *Avalanche*). At one stage Kesselring was nearly proved right as the grip on the Salerno beaches appeared almost tenuous, and at times it looked as if the landing might fail. At Salerno General Mark Clark had decided not to prepare his landing beaches with naval fire as he thought the landing would be a surprise, but it was already a well broadcast invasion.* Later Eisenhower admitted that the American commanders at Salerno 'lacked skills', and Alexander admitted the British and Americans 'did not get along'.[27] Another error in the Salerno landing was the belief the Italians would welcome them with open arms, neglecting the possibility that the greeting would be a German defence and attack. Salerno with its hinterland was tough, *The Times* grudgingly admitted that in Italy 'the German resistance has been skilful, stubborn, and fierce … most of his [Kesselring] divisions are of high quality…some are exceptionally good… and his engineers have shown their customary skill'.[28] It was Kesselring's able defence which influenced Hitler to accept Kesselring's policy of a fighting defence from the toe of Italy all the way up the Italian peninsula, and favouring Kesselring's strategy to that of Rommel's. There had been the Allied hope that after the fall of Naples, Rome would fall with the help of the Italians, but Kesselring was no fool, and slowly German troops had infiltrated Rome which remained in German control, and well defended south by the Gustav line.

* As soldiers embarked in North African street vendors were selling postcards of Salerno.

Von Senger drove with his batman and a friend called Rohr up through Italy as if on holiday and enjoyed the sights of the Italian countryside, then to Munich, where there was no news of a new appointment, so he took a train home to Göttingen.

Later he reflected on his war to date in Italy, realising that his sole postings had been about evacuating troops from the three islands of Sicily, Sardinia, and Corsica. He ruminated on the nature of the insular aspect of island peoples, noting how the three major islands off Italy's west coast had always been subject to attack, vacillating between Italian, French and Spanish occupation, spending several thousands of words giving his readers various insights into Mediterranean island life. He then turned his study to the geographical nature of the islands as well as the sociological attitudes, stating the better educated lived in the coastal towns, the lack of constitutional status, the complexities of mixed languages, the development of blood-feuds, and the way island people tended to see 'foreigners with passive indifference', and cared little about what was happening on mainland Europe, which may have rung bells if written over half a century later during the British Brexit debate.

He spent more time on the operational significance of the islands, looking at the significant differences of opinion between the Allied choice of Sicily or Sardinia which divided opinion within the Allied camp, with the same speculation amongst the Axis strategists. He weighed up the better aerodrome places in Sardinia and Corsica, but their ports were not so good, and they were probably too close to the Luftwaffe main sites. He knew that Salerno beach was probably chosen for Allied air cover, but he did not mention that in Salerno the Germans had the high ground [which Mark Clark later admitted when he flew over it after the battle] and at one time it looked as if the invasion would fail.

Von Senger's memoirs are unusual as he spends considerable time on such reflections with the benefit of hindsight and discussion long after the war had finished, even having read Mark Clark's biography. This was because he was at heart a thinking intellectual who, having found himself in a military career because of the 1914–18 war, had turned his interest to tactics and the strategy of war. Kesselring had probably realised his abilities because of his accurate forecasts while in Sicily, but this did not seem to have permeated the High Command who had given him somewhat ambiguous roles in his Mediterranean island hopping, often just a liaison officer, and ordered to evacuate troops, not lead them to advance. Nevertheless, he had accomplished the evacuation of Sardinia and Corsica, and this had been recognised. There may have been doubts about his political views, and this must have crossed his mind when arriving at Munich and hearing no news of a new appointment. His next appointment was therefore pleasing when he was told he was returning to Italy with the command of the XIV Panzer Corps, and not some form of liaison officer.

Chapter 4

The Italian Campaign

Bernhardt Line, Commanding XIV Panzer Corps

As far as von Senger was concerned he saw this as a return to a normal appointment as he was directly in charge of troops. He was, he discovered, to be responsible for a vast tract of the western front north of Naples and south of Rome, and his main opponent was the American 5th Army under General Mark Clark. He found his corps headquarters in the main HQ at Roccasecca, many of the officers he knew from his time in Sicily. It was at first a curious meeting because the internal military politics emerged with many there strongly supportive of Rommel and less so of Kesselring. Many of these were North African veterans and believers in Rommel's leadership qualities, while feeling that Kesselring had let them down. Von Senger decided, that having not been in North Africa, he was no judge of their views. He expressed what he felt about Kesselring having worked with him in Sicily and Corsica, namely that his well-known optimism and belief in Hitler were not propelled by ambition but from his own inbuilt convictions, which he saw as Kesselring's driving force. He also gathered that Rommel was convinced the war was lost, whereas Kesselring was always optimistic, and later stood in defence on the western front until the very last days. There was also the added controversy between Rommel and Kesselring as to the strategy of defence in Italy. From the very start Kesselring had made it clear that in his opinion, as mentioned above, the defence should be metre by metre from the south to the north. Rommel wanted to make a stand in the north on the Gothic Line, and generally it appeared the vacillating Hitler favoured Kesselring's approach. Kesselring saw strong defence Lines as critical to avoid a hasty withdrawal north to the Apennine mountains, and if necessary, gain time for building the defence in that area. Von Senger's Chief of Staff, a pro-Rommel man regarded Kesselring's delaying defence as letting down the troops, and they were all frustrated by not having direct strategic policies from High Command (OKW). Von Senger was pleased, however, to find that General Heinrich von Vietinghoff and General Siegfried Westphal serving with him under Kesselring were both men he admired for different reasons. He was like the others somewhat frustrated by the lack of High Command communication, as it was uncertain whether Kesselring's policy of a resolute defence south of Rome was essential or a move towards the Apennines, because these two policies needed different tactics. Roccasecca was a medieval town hidden high at the head of the Liri valley, with Rome only 75 miles away, with views across the open countryside to the Liri river joining the Rapido river just 15 miles away.

As it stood, when he arrived, it was a matter of defending the Bernhardt Line sometimes called the Reinhard Line (known to the Allies as the Winter Line), and to hold it as long as possible. If this Line were not held, the next Line north and still south of Rome was the Gustav Line. Von Senger believed the Bernhardt Line had its weaknesses as it was dominated by high peaks. What von Senger did not mention at this stage was the professional tactical approach the German commanders took by often taking the high ground, especially those overlooking roads and rivers, and by using a few heavy machine guns and other weapons hidden in the mountain gullies they could dominate the valleys below. Von Senger's other concern was that the enemy had the ability and resources to make a coastal landing north of the defence lines, so the Germans were badly stretched looking out for such an incursion to happen, which it eventually did. Applying his usual vigour in trying to weigh up the situation, von Senger noted where the various units and who commanded them were situated.

Curiously he came upon one racial problem he knew was wrong. There were men called *Volksdeutschen* who had come from the occupied zones of Poland. They could earn decorations for bravery, but they were not offered any advancement until a period of probation had been concluded. Von Senger saw this as 'discriminatory' and not helping the morale of the troops. He also gathered that their letters from home could be upsetting as families complained they were being ill-treated by Nazi Party members. There is little doubt that von Senger was viewing this problem from two angles. The first was the need for morale amongst the fighting troops, and the word 'racial' clearly indicated his moral stance on treating people differently because of their nationality or colour. These men belonged to the 3rd Panzer Grenadiers and because of their circumstances von Senger was concerned about their fighting ability.[1]

Another problem he discovered was not knowing enough about the enemy they faced. Such was the terrain it was a difficult or even impossible task to send out recce groups, and they had to rely upon any prisoners they were able to capture. He travelled up to the frontline posts to see for himself the nature of the situation. The word Line was something of a misnomer, it was not like the Maginot or Seigfried lines of connected defences, merely a line of gun and machine gun emplacements spread for example across a ridge or mountain, or a top of a hill providing good observation points. It was becoming clear to both sides that the terrain was better for defence than attack. Some had been reinforced but many were makeshift hideaways chosen for space and appropriate rock formations for concealing soldiers and their guns. The word Line was more appropriate for a map showing the defence positions and drawing a pencil line between them.

Like all the best military commanders he made a point of visiting the various posts which constituted the so-called defence Line, the first one being at Pozzilli (a small commune in Province of Isernia). It was like so many designated points of defence in the line and felt to von Senger as somewhat pointless. He reflected on the defence lines in Russia where the Todt organisation had at least managed to construct defence positions by using slave labour, but as in Russia, so in Italy, it was impossible to link them, making the word Line something of a misnomer. In addition to this he noted that as in Russia finding accommodation was not easy. The winter in Russia had been extreme, but as von Senger noted the winter in the Italian mountains was extremely tough. He recalled that most Germans associated Italy with holiday climates and sunny beaches, not rain drenched and freezing cold valleys and mountains. He may have been bemused to know that the same problems related to the Allied planners whose knowledge of the terrain and climate was limited. Postwar it was realised that the Italian terrain of mountains, rivers, valleys, and winter weather had provided Kesselring with the best defensive measures; it was the Allies who had the difficult task. In addition to this 'modern artillery and the invention of the machine gun meant there was a relative shift to the power of defence on the battlefield'.[2] It has been described as a 'military campaign of consummate strategic stupidity – an offensive up the entire length of a long, thin, mountainous country'.[3] Despite von Senger's critique of the defence lines, Kesselring had the terrain on his side; Italy was long, narrow, mountainous, with narrow roads and cold winters and was easier to defend than to attack. Ernie Pyle the war correspondent wrote that:

> The war in Italy was tough. The land and the weather were both against us. It rained and it rained. Vehicles bogged down and temporary bridges washed out. The country was shockingly beautiful, and just as shockingly hard to capture from the enemy. The hills rose to high ridges of almost solid rock. We couldn't go round them through the flat peaceful valleys, because the Germans were up there looking down upon us, and they would have let us have it. So, we had to go up and over. A mere platoon of Germans, well dug in on high, rock-spined hill, could hold out for a long time against tremendous onslaughts.[4]

Von Senger, 'more than any other man, was responsible for stopping Clark's advancing army' which is overlooked in many histories.[5] Von Senger also noted that the fighting qualities of the Americans had vastly improved since he had seen them in Sicily. This inexperience in war had first come to light in North Africa of which von Senger had no experience. Kesselring had already suspected that the American troops were inexperienced. Eisenhower admitted his troops were unprepared especially after the battle for the Kasserine Pass in North Africa, even finding engineers ordered to dig into rock to give cover for senior officers, writing that 'it was the only time, during the war, that I saw a divisional or higher headquarters so concerned over its own safety that it dug itself underground shelters'.[6] The blame for the Kasserine Pass one historian wrote 'must be shared by Anderson, Eisenhower and Fredendall' and led to the humiliating spectacle of some 4,000 Allied PoWs being marched through Rome.[7] However, not only did the Germans justifiably pride themselves on a highly professional army, but they had been fighting for years, whereas for American soldiers and commanders alike the reality of battle had been a novelty in North Africa and to a degree in Sicily. Eisenhower, amongst the reasons he listed for failure, noted 'greenness, particularly among commanders', as well as the failure to comprehend the capability of the enemy.[8] Von Senger was correct, after the mainland invasion and the battle on the Salerno beaches the Americans had become, as von Senger noted, good in attacking, writing that 'evidently the Americans were no longer affected by the novelty of battle'. Von Senger was shocked when he heard that German troops in a forward position on Monte Cesima had been thrown back, and a German parachute rifle battalion had failed to recapture the position. The Allied attacks were becoming more successful, and von Senger could see that key points were being lost on the Bernhardt Line. None of this was helped by the narrow roads and passes needed to bring ammunition and weapons to the remote points in the Line. Von Senger noted that by the end of November (1943) the Bernhardt Line had not only been dented in the centre but to the north.

He was concerned about a new Division (Reichsgrenadier-Division Hoch-und Deutschmeister) from Vienna, not only because they were inexperienced, but that they had been raised in Austria, an annexed country, and not from Germany which had voted Hitler to power. For some critics this would have been a curious viewpoint because in Germany there were a growing number of citizens, including von Senger, who were either critical of Hitler or some who opposed him. Whereas in Vienna, there had been some who wanted the annexation and many who were already dedicated Nazis. This attitude by von Senger may offer an insight into his political thinking as to why an educated and intellectually gifted man like von Senger who had no time for Hitler and disobeyed some of the tyrant's criminal orders should continue to serve him. This aspect of von Senger will be further explored in the final chapter.

As preparations were made to fall back to the Gustav Line, von Senger decided to see for himself the situation on the two high points they still held, choosing Monte Samucro (2 December), and while descending saw for himself the bombardment and shelling in the area which was worse than he had experienced during the Great War. At the top of Monte Camino, they seemed to be holding their own, but when a runner was sent up to view the situation all he found was corpses. According to von Senger there followed some bitter arguments with the OKW over the permission for withdrawal. The conflict between commanders on the front line with high command hundreds of miles away was well known, not only in Germany but also on the Allied side. In Britain, Churchill was forever debating with his Chief of the Imperial General Staff General Brooke, who always insisted Churchill should leave decision making to the commanders on the front line. Later when the Allies did as von Senger feared and launched another coastal invasion in the north, the British Chief of the Imperial Staff, General Brooke 'attended a Joint Intelligence Committee meeting and learnt that Alexander had launched, or rather ordered the Anzio beachhead breakout, and wondered whether he was too soon, but decided to stick by his policy, which he had always upheld with Churchill, to trust the commander on the front line'.[9] There had been constant debates between Brooke and Churchill over the necessity of trusting commanders on the spot to make the right decision because they could see what was happening. Brooke tended to win, but on the German side the OKW often had to reflect Hitler's viewpoint which was often warped. This often led to what von Senger feared most, namely the command to fight to the last man. In this case the OKW eventually agreed to withdrawal but at the very last moment. The word 'withdrawal' was preferred to 'retreat'. Annoyingly for von Senger army regulations demanded he should start an official enquiry over the loss of equipment, which he knew at ground level had to happen when life was endangered. Near the end of December, they also lost the other high point on Monte Samucro, and generally von Senger could see that further prolonged resistance in that area was fruitless, and at last a retreat to the Gustav Line was agreed, but bitter fighting continued to enable the withdrawal to take place. Once again, von Senger was concerned about the Allied air support over Italy's battlefields, and especially at the later Anzio landing. What planes the Luftwaffe had were used effectively, especially in shipping attacks with the new radio-guided bomb.* Von Senger admitted the air attacks on their supply lines were disturbing, but they were never cut, and the aircraft came at enormous costs: 'some 315,000 men were needed

* Fritz X – it sank the Italian flagship *Roma* and disabled American warships at Salerno.

to keep those thousands of aircraft operational – almost as many as the 5th or 8th Army'.[10] It should also be noted that aircraft were frequently grounded because of 'appalling weather conditions', and Anzio would not have survived without air support.[11] Regarding the Gustav line Churchill saw the 'air offensive as a failure'.[12]

Gustav Line, Monte Cassino

On Christmas Day von Senger was able to attend Mass in the crypt of Monte Cassino Abbey, and one historian noted that he had first asked permission from the Abbot, and he did not just walk in.[13] He was the only officer to do so, and he placed a sentry at the door to ensure soldiers did not wander in as would be tourists. Von Senger does not appear to claim this was his policy to safeguard the monastery, though it may have been him who influenced Kesselring to make this decision, which later created mayhem for the Allies during the war and postwar as this account unfolds. To enter the Abbey, he devised the excuse he was checking that the promise was being maintained, but it was known he frequently attended to make his communion.

Even at this stage of arriving at the Gustav Line he noticed from the heights of the Abbey that the whole valley was filled with harassing fire which continued throughout the night. Von Senger thought the battle scenario was very different from the more mobile battles of Russia, more like the trench warfare of the First World War. He re-organised the various corps and the 29 Panzer Grenadier Division, because he needed reserves to protect the Liri valley which led to Rome. This writer in 2010 walked part of the Gustav line west into Monte Cassino and was simply astounded by the dominating hills. It clearly indicated that the Allies, despite superior resources and stronger logistics, had a difficult time attacking Germans who knew that dominating the high ground made for a more effective defence. The area was so steep and mountainous that von Senger knew mountain troops would be better for dealing with that environment but bringing them in from Russia was virtually out of the question, and there were only two railway lines capable of such action, especially with the dominating Allied air power. It appeared that Kesselring managed to convince the Führer for the transfer of 5 Mountain

Group, but like many they were disappointed when they arrived that it was not the anticipated sunny climes. In the freezing high mountains of the Abruzzi region even these troops had to descend towards the enemy for the sake of survival.

The persistent problem which dominated the various commanders' discussions was how to withdraw from their old strongholds while at the same time building up the Gustav Line positions. Von Senger was concerned to find the new mountain troops were not that experienced, and they were facing French troops under General Pierre Juin (who in 1952 was made Marshal of France) whose soldiers were mainly Moroccan and Algerian, born and bred in mountains but now equipped with the latest American weapons, thus making them formidable opponents. It also transpired that they were especially powerful in sharp brutal forays which gave a sense of fear to those fighting them. As the Bernhardt Line slowly became a figure of history, it was a time of considerable worry and concern for von Senger and his colleagues, as they tried to ensure their new positions were not only in the best tactical places, but resourced and with men capable of withstanding an immediate attack. This happened on 18 January which the Allies had hoped would break all German resistance, opening the way through the Liri Valley using their army towards their target of Rome. It was known as the First Battle of Cassino. Von Senger could see the Allies were using several points of attack from various directions, some more concerning than others. The defence was not helped by the unfavourable terrain according to von Senger, but it was this singular geographical issue which made it difficult for the Allies, especially having to cross the Garigliano and Sangro rivers which the Germans knew were essential and well defended. Von Senger had limited artillery and needed more, but the major task was the vast width of area which had to be fortified, especially being so dependent upon infantry. Von Senger asked Kesselring for two extra divisions and was pleased if somewhat surprised that he agreed for two Panzer Grenadier Divisions stationed in Rome to be allocated, obviously hoping that the Gustav Line would stabilise the front. For von Senger this was essential because he had worked out that the enemy were trying to outflank him.

Between 20 and 22 January Clark's forces were trying to cross the Gari where the Allied forces suffered a serious hammer blow. It was von Senger's responsibility to hold the lines at the Rapido river and Liri Valley.[14] Von Senger's memoirs pass over this battle fairly swiftly, with him noting that the enemy suffered 400 dead and the Germans taking some 500 prisoners. The battle of crossing the river was highly significant and was better known in the Western Allied camp as the Rapido disaster. The Rapido was a part of the Gari River which Senger had well-fortified from higher ground. Kesselring had competent commanders, not least von Senger, but also his Chief of Staff Westphal, General Vietinghoff was back in command of the 10th Army, with Mackensen as commander of the newly formed 14th Army.* After the British widened the bridgehead at the Garigliano, and the American 36th Division arrived at the Rapido they were met by heavy German artillery. The German resistance was strong, and Field Marshal Alexander wrote to Churchill that 'the Germans are fighting magnificently. Never imagine they are crashing. Their staff work is brilliantly flexible'.[15] However, there was poor planning by the American General Mark Clark which led to sheer slaughter, and 'the officers and men of the 36th Division were unequivocal as to who was responsible, it was entirely Mark Clark's fault'.[16] There were some persuasive arguments that the disaster was the responsibility of the local commander General Walker, but either way the Allies made it easier for von Senger and his men to defend and earn Alexander's praise.[17] It was because of the holdup at Monte Cassino, and Clark knowing that in a few days the Anzio (22 January) landing would take place at Nettuno north of Monte Cassino, which had prompted Clark to make the demands for a greater pace from his troops which led to the disaster at the Rapido River.

Curiously, in his diary Clark barely mentions the Rapido disaster although his demands for this venture were to haunt him long after the war, and as von Senger mentioned in his memoirs led to a Congressional enquiry. 'The Rapido River became and would remain a dark cloud over the reputation of Mark Clark', who had he any real combat experience would have taken heed of his subordinate officers warning him of the high ground occupied by battle-hardened German soldiers.[18] In his diary Clark mentioned sending his chief-of-staff General Gruenther to see General McCreery, who had told Clark's emissary that the 36th

* Friedrich von Mackensen (1889–1969), son of the famous Field Marshal August von Mackenson.

Division had little chance of success at the Rapido because the river was dominated by high ground held by the Germans. Clark's response was instant, stating that the attack must be done even though 'fully expecting heavy losses in order to hold all the troops on my front and draw more to it, thereby clearing the way for [Operation] *Shingle*. The attack is on.'[19]

General Walker wrote in his diary that 'this is going to be a tough job and I don't like it. There is nothing in our favour' and he suggested to Clark an attack further north but 'Clark and Keyes are not interested. They do not understand the problems and do not know what I am talking about'.[20] Later adding 'that the Army has rushed us into this mission too fast…even with adequate time, the crossing is still dominated by heights on both sides of the valley'.[21] Walker later added the note that 'there are times when the high command is as stupid as hell'.[22]

As a result of Clark's insistence, during the failed Rapido crossing the 36th Division suffered 1,681 casualties, 143 deaths, 663 wounded and 875 missing.[23] All Clark noted in his diary was that 'heavy resistance to the 36th Division crossing river' with no further comment.[24] He tried to explain it by claiming he thought it better for the 'Allies to face a critical situation at the Rapido than with their backs to the sea'.[25]

The Congressional Inquiry mentioned by von Senger was held on 20 January 1946, less than a year after the war had finished. The men of the 36th petitioned the 'Congress to investigate the river Rapido fiasco and take the necessary steps to correct a military system that will permit an inefficient and inexperienced officer, such as General Mark W. Clark, in a high command to destroy the young manhood of this country and to prevent future soldiers being sacrificed wastefully and uselessly'. It was too soon after the final victory for the House of Representatives to do anything but absolve Clark as heroes were badly needed. Clark barely mentioned the Rapido battle in his own writings, probably because one of the resolutions heard in the House of Representatives stated that it was 'one of the most colossal blunders of the Second World War'.

On reading his memoirs Clark skilfully moved through this difficult issue by first mentioning the British 46th Division failure, (whereas von Senger had not seen the British effort in this light) caused by a 'lack of strong aggressive leadership' which created 'strong enemy positions along the Rapido'.[26] Clark was intensely Anglophobic and blaming the

British was his common habit. He then swiftly moved to the controversy that he had been under 'strong political pressure' and that Anzio was so essential the Rapido crossing was necessary. He paid little credit to the Germans, and probably never knew that it had been von Senger who had persuaded Kesselring for the extra divisions. For the Americans it was a humiliating disaster, for von Senger it was no more than another action in the desperate bid to hold the Gustav Line as long as possible, admitting that the terrain was more familiar to the German forces than it was to the Allies. It was only after the war that von Senger appeared to realise the damage this conflict at the Rapido had caused, because at this time news had come through of the Allied landing on the Nettuno beaches under General John Lucas.

The battleground of Italy had become a series of focal points which have since become household names. First Operation *Baytown* when Montgomery landed on the deserted toe of Italy, followed by Salerno, Operation *Avalanche*, after which the Allies pressed north through heavily defended river crossings until they came upon the Gustav Line with its pivotal point at Cassino. The nature of the mountainous terrain demanded more amphibious landings, and although Kesselring believed the Allies would carry out another invasion Anzio (Operation *Shingle*) still took him by surprise. He had preparatory plans, namely Operation *Richard*, which entailed having reserve divisions ready to swing into action across the breadth of Italy. Even after Anzio he remained convinced, with Allied deception, that there would be another landing around Leghorn. The Allies planned two major advances: General Clark's 5th Army in the west to enter the Liri Valley after eliminating Monte Cassino; Montgomery's 8th Army along the Adriatic; and Kesselring's reserves would be rushed from one to the other coast as and when necessary. The Anzio landing was the expected shock von Senger and Kesselring had dreaded, but as von Senger noted they landed but found themselves battened down on the beach for months. News of the landings had reached Kesselring by 3am, by 5am troops were heading to the beach, and by 7.10am orders were given for northern reserves to move south. Kesselring flew to the front in the early morning and returned late evening to avoid Allied aircraft.[27]

Churchill was furious and known for saying that he thought they had landed a 'wild cat' but instead it was a 'beached whale'. The speed of

Kesselring's reaction indicated his highly professional approach, and it has been pointed out that 'the Germans produced seven Divisions in ten days with plenty of armour'.[28] The Anzio beachhead seemed frozen and 'Kesselring used this hiatus to create a new defensive line, the Caesar C Line, to contain the beachhead'.[29] For the next few months the whole landing appeared trapped and somewhat tenuous, and by mid-May there were an estimated 150,000 men on the beachhead, eventually breaking out by the end of May.

Back in Cassino, von Senger was facing a third assault this time to the north of his lines, a long bitter assault where the US 34 Division managed to make some formidable penetrations with the French Corps, with von Senger pointing out the tough fighting spirit of the French Colonial troops. As far as von Senger could see these French troops were better than his own. They could have, at this time, penetrated the town of Cassino, but von Senger was able to reinforce the German side with the newly arrived divisions. Nevertheless, the enemy made a successful attempt and took the hills to the north-west of the town, which overlooked the only reasonable road to Cassino. Von Senger was caught between the deep blue sea and the devil, as the attacks from the south were still strong but the incursions from the north hinted that this may be the critical point for their main effort. He climbed to a point still held by his troops and found a spot for their artillery, which helped hold the defence.

Having secured the lines he suggested to Kesselring that they withdrew from Cassino and establish a defence line further north, which Kesselring had designated the C (Caesar) Line, which was behind the Nettuno bridgehead, and thereby avoid the inevitable loss of German units to the south. It was promptly refused but he took heart in that it appeared the enemy was declining in strength, and later he criticised the way the Allies had handled their tactics. He could not understand why the enemy tried to break through at so many points, because his own training indicated that it dissipated their forces. After the war he met the British General McCreery and the American General Keyes and discussed their plans, understood their points of view but still disagreed. It must have felt for a time that the area was almost at peace as the intensity of the fighting had slowed down.

In May the Allies started to increase their pressure to the south, he was aware that the New Zealand Corps had been brought up, but his main fear was an incursion by the French Colonial troops who were widely feared. He later realised that his portion of troops covered a wide span, from the coast into the heights of the Abruzzi area. His communications were critical, and covering such a wide area made him feel like a director of operations. He had his accommodation in a run-down *Palazzo* in Roccasecca, and his major enjoyment was strolling in the countryside as and when it was safe. Some areas and some roads were dangerous being under constant attack any time movement was detected. Von Senger, being the character he was, spent considerable time in his memoirs reflecting on past battles which had been fought in the same area, including wars by the Spanish and French, even down to the fact they had crossed the same rivers in the same places as had the current Allies. He eventually had to change his headquarters to Castell Massimo which was more secluded and quieter. He also had a change of personal staff, with a new Chief-of-Staff, a Colonel Schmidt von Altenstadt, where being smaller in number, he was able to talk more freely and found to his delight they had similar political views. It was here he discovered von Altenstadt was a friend of Count von Stauffenberg, and that he was working with certain commanders for the overthrow of Adolf Hitler. His GSO1 (General Staff Officer Grade 1) was the son of General Hans Oster (Abwehr) who was one of the most dedicated resisters to Nazism. Sadly, as a consequence of this resistance, Oster's son, von Senger's friend, was caught up in the aftermath of revenge. The Nazis had re-adopted the medieval policy of prosecuting (persecuting) kith and kin. It was this fear which often meant that even the most active resisters had to walk a tight-rope and not be seen conversing or attending meetings with the ever-observant Gestapo and their informers, making any resistance dangerous. In Nazi Germany there was no form of immunity they could rely on, as Field Marshal Rommel had to face much later. It was well known that von Senger liked and enjoyed the company of his subordinates, not least General Baade whom he had worked with in Sicily and mainland Italy. He would also have been aware that Baade had no liking for the Nazi regime.

Von Senger was pleased to be in the company of men who were prepared to talk about their disgust of the Nazi regime and its political party (NSDAP) which brought Hitler to power. There was for von Senger a great relief to be surrounded by staff who were not engrossed with criticising Kesselring while supporting Rommel and accepting Hitler as the overall leader. His previous staff had taken setbacks as due to the faults of third parties. They had assumed that failures were a means of insulting the Führer, blaming him as the cause of the problems, daring to suggest he was not the genius that he and many other senior military commanders believed. Von Senger and his newly acquired staff, like many other more astute military commanders knew the war could no longer be won and would be lost. Von Senger's only difference with his new cabal was that he could not foresee Hitler being overthrown, whereas they were certain it would happen. He was also concerned that the war was being won by Russia and that Russia would, as a consequence, rule defeated Germany. He did not add the possibility that under Stalin they may have moved west of Germany on the excuse of cleansing Europe of Nazism. These memoirs were written in the 1950s during the heightening of the Cold War, and it is not ascertainable whether these thoughts reflected his postwar thinking or his fears in 1944. He even pondered that because of this possibility, his own defence system was hindering the Allies of breaking through before the Russians. Another matter he and his new staff agreed upon was the abominable treatment of Jews by the Nazi masters. They confessed to feeling ashamed the way the 'intellectually gifted minority of the population' had been treated. He recognised the fact that the habitual anti-Semitism had degenerated into murder. To his further delight he found that General Heinrich von Vietinghoff, whom he saw more of, also held similar views.

Bombing of the Abbey

The Gustav Line was a series of battles, but the Allied victory on Monte Cassino was elusive and cost many lives. The massive hill on which the Abbey stood could be described as a mountain and was heavily defended, and 'in November the Germans had put 100 steel shelters into the Cassino position, and they added more later, as well as 76 armoured casements and a number of armoured machine-gun nests'.[30] Kesselring admitted the use of the 'natural features with concrete armoured positions and enfilading fire' made defence easier than attack.[31] The bombing of the Abbey by the Allies caused considerable reaction on a global basis, not only at the time but postwar, and remains contentious to this day. Before commenting on von Senger's views it was felt best by the writer to take time to explore as objectively as humanly possible what happened, by exploring the wide and various historical accounts. It was extremely unlikely that the Germans used the Abbey despite the occasional spotter-plane observations and the claims of misunderstood radio-messages. Kesselring had refused the use of the Abbey having 'given his assurance to the Vatican on the 11 December 1943', and since then many times confirmed, especially by von Senger and the Monastery's Abbot.[32]

Who originally came up with the idea of bombing one of the most famous and ancient sites in Italy (which Kesselring had once described as like fighting in a museum) will always be difficult to fathom out, and not helped postwar as the Allied participants have made various efforts to distance themselves from the decision making.

On 3 February Field Marshal Alexander ordered the New Zealand 2nd Division and the 4th Indian Division under General Freyberg to join General Clark's 5th Army. Freyberg believed that Cassino and its surrounds were inviolate unless the Abbey were destroyed: he was convinced the Abbey was an observation point and demanded its destruction; this drastic thinking may have been influenced when he heard that his only son was missing at Anzio.[33] However, the bombing destruction of the Abbey has had many indicators to its origins and such a major decision is unlikely to have rested solely on the New Zealander Freyberg, but many influences and opinions were brought to bear. As in most postwar analysis of battles there were division of opinions, claims and counterclaims that continued after the war. There were those who argued Monte Cassino could be outflanked, including Major-General Tuker and the French Commander Juin.* Tuker claimed Freyburg 'should never have been put in charge of a corps, he did not have the tactical understanding'; he nevertheless had Alexander's support.[34] 'Tuker could

* Edwin Hoyt, *Back Water War: The Allied Campaign in Italy* (Mechanicsburg: Stackpole, 2007), p.159 claims it was Tuker who asked Freyberg to bomb the abbey and recently two New Zealand historians have also claimed the same, Harper & Tonkin-Covell, *The Battles of Monte Cassino: The Campaign and its Controversies* (Auckland: Allen & Unwin, 2013), p.16.

not understand why Cassino town, monastery and point 593 be made point of attack' unless the bombing would ensure the total destruction of resistance, otherwise it was possible to outflank along the northern route and Garigliano River, writing 'I went on arguing this from hospital by letter through my divisional headquarters'.[35]

In his memoirs Alexander wrote that a misinterpretation of a German radio message prompted the Allies to think the Germans were inside the Abbey. He wrote that it was 'a curious and slightly comical incident... an American officer picked up on the wireless...conclusive proof that the Germans were inside the monastery. The interpreted conversation ran: "*Wo ist der Abt? Ist er noch im Kloste,*" *Abt* is the Germany military abbreviation for *Abteilung* meaning a section. Unfortunately, *Abt* also means Abbot, and since *Abt* is masculine and *abteilung* feminine, the conversation referred to the Abbot...a little knowledge of a foreign tongue can be a dangerous thing'.[36]

It was unlikely that the Germans used the Abbey despite what the occasional spotter-plane and misunderstood radio-messages claimed. That Kesselring had refused the use of the Abbey, having 'given his assurance to the Vatican on 11 December 1943, was confirmed by Westphal, and as von Senger noted the Abbey was cordoned off by military police for its protection.[37] The Abbot said the Germans had not broken the agreement; the Abbot's secretary, Don Martino Matronola's diary recorded that the Germans never entered the premises.[38] Von Senger, as a Lay-Benedictine attended mass and said he was the only German present; and even Churchill later admitted that the evidence indicated there were no Germans.[39]

The military theorist J.C.F. Fuller described the bombing as 'not so much a piece of vandalism as an act of sheer tactical stupidity'.[40] The Germans, as noted, had dug in below the buildings on that formidable hill, and the antiquity of the religious site was a secondary consideration to Freyberg and Eisenhower who decided human life was more important; yet they were aware 'that as many as 3,000 Italian civilians had sought shelter within the monastery's walls', believing that there existed some form of agreement between the two sides to leave the monastery safe.[41] The Germans had declared a 300 metre wide non-combat zone around the abbey, which in terms of the sharp decline was still within the shadows of the walls. To preserve the Abbey meant avoiding the mountain, but it was militarily out of the question for the Germans, so whether the monastery was occupied or not was a fatuous debate because Monte Cassino dominated the area, and even if they had declared it an 'open site' that would not bind the Allies, making it a highly confusing issue.*

On the morning of 15 February 96 Bombardment Group in Foggia read their brief which stated that the Abbey 'is a huge ancient monastery which the Germans have chosen as a key defence and have loaded with heavy guns ... the monastery has accounted for the lives of upwards of 2,000 American boys who felt the same as we do about church property and who paid for it because the Germans do not understand anything human when total war is concerned. The monastery MUST be destroyed and everyone in it as there is no one in but Germans'.[42] Later that day over 400 tons of bombs were dropped on the Abbey killing sheltering Italian civilians and monks, and totally destroying the buildings: according to von Senger no German was killed.**

The bombing was and will always remain contentious and gave the Germans a means of making propaganda from what was regarded as a 'Philistine' act. A Berlin diarist wrote that 'photographs of the battle of Monte Cassino are piling up. The destruction of that beautiful monastery is horrifying. What will happen to Florence, Venice, Rome?'[43] In Dublin de Valera took advantage to send an appeal to the belligerent governments and to Roosevelt personally on behalf of Rome.[44] Kesselring later in his own memoirs noted that aerial attack 'was not only quite unnecessary but prejudicial to the subsequent conduct of the battle'.[45] German parachutists, led by Major Rudolf Bohmler, used the rubble as a form of ideal defence. Von Senger wrote, 'now we would occupy the abbey without scruple, especially as ruins are better for defence than intact buildings'.[46] Bohmler later wrote that if the Allies had attacked immediately with a flanking movement, they would have won the hill, but the paratroopers had time to turn the rubble into a fortress.[47] It has been noted that from the Allied perspective 'there did not appear to be a glimmer of intelligent leadership anywhere from division up'.[48] The historian Ellis in his book on Monte Cassino concludes with the powerful indictment that both the 5th and

---

* Today the Abbey sells an account and castigates the Allies for the destruction.

** In the morning 257 tons of 500 lb bombs, 59 tons of 100 lb incendiaries; in the afternoon 283 tons each weighing 1,000 lbs.

8th armies were 'poorly led during the Cassino battles'.[49] The bombing which created defensive strong points and the late, untimed, infantry attack were indicators of this poor planning, and made the German defence easier.

The debate will undoubtedly continue: the Germans appeared to respect the Abbey and its treasures, but they could not ignore the dominating mountain on which the Abbey stood, and the non-combat zone was pointless. The Allies were right to place lives before ancient monuments, but the bombing provided excellent defensive rubble for the paratroopers. Monte Cassino had an effect in that property of an historic nature such as the Ponte Vecchio in Florence and Venice were spared by Kesselring, and on 17 February, just a few days after the bombing, Alexander sent a belated letter to commanders about preserving 'property of historical and educational importance in Italy'.[50] In the postwar period the debate intensified with Clark claiming he was always against the venture, but Freyberg, then New Zealand's Governor-General in a letter to Kippenberger, wrote that Clark had said 'nothing would do but to bring in the heavy fortresses'.[51] Personality conflict in the Allied coalition during and after the war assisted Kesselring. It has been argued that von Senger could have done more to protect the Abbey based on the grounds argued by General Ira Eaker noting that from the walls 'I could have dropped my binoculars into a machine-gun nest less than 50 feet from the walls'.[52] In terms of the 300 metre boundary round the walls it was not a genuine safeguard, especially when von Senger's headquarters later 'issued an order to the 44th Infantry Division to evacuate civilians as soon as possible, and make no use of the abbey buildings, but make defences right up to the abbey wall if necessary'.[53] Von Senger had no choice but to put military priorities first, and it is noticeable that he never mentioned the 300 zone in his memoirs, probably out of personal embarrassment. It has often been pointed out by military experts and historians that any use of the Abbey hill by the defenders put the monastery at risk. Even in his war diary many are quick to note that von Senger appeared to accept that ancient monuments were less important than human lives.[54]

The bombing was a vexed and complex problem, and the reader of these accounts, like the writer, might wonder where they stood on the issue if they had been part of the attacking forces. Either way, 'all 22,000 citizens had fled or died, ceding the cobbled streets to General von Senger and German paratroopers in their brimless helmets, who in late February replaced the Panzer Grenadiers previously holding the Gustav Line', and the battle continued into what has been seen as one of the most stubborn defences under von Senger's tactics and control.[55]

On Wednesday 15 March there was another bombing raid on Monte Cassino. Over 1,400 bombs were dropped, but because of the safety of the rubble from the initial raid, the parachutists were dug in, and although they could only move at night, they still managed a formidable resistance. Churchill complained about the failure to take Monte Cassino to Alexander, who in his reply wrote that lack of success was that the 'the tenacity of these German paratroopers is quite remarkable .... I doubt if there are any other troops in the world who could have stood up to it and then gone on fighting with the ferocity they have'.[56] Despite warnings from General Ira Eaker of the USAAF, the rubble created by the bombing stopped the use of tanks, and yet again the infantry was sent in late, they 'dribbled in' according to Kippenberger.[57]

It would appear the Allies failed at this juncture to use their air supremacy appropriately, and it was 'sadly inadequate'.[58] The actual bombing raid on Cassino town damaged towns away from Cassino and killed Allied troops, hitting the '8th Army HQ, General Juin's FEC HQ, Allied gun-positions, the 4th Indian Division's B Echelon and the Moroccan military hospital'.[59] Von Senger admitted the air attacks on their supply lines were disturbing, but they were never cut, and the aircraft came at enormous costs: 'some 315,000 men were needed to keep those thousands of aircraft operational...almost as many as the 5th or 8th Army'.[60] It should also be noted that aircraft were frequently grounded because of the 'appalling weather conditions', and Anzio would not have survived without air support.[61] Regarding the Gustav line even Churchill saw the 'air offensive as a failure'.[62]

Alexander wanted to stop the frontal attacks, but Freyberg was insistent they could win, but on 23 March Alexander called off frontal attacks for a time. 'The performance of commanders is critical to the outcome of any conflict' and this was more than apparent at Monte Cassino.[63] The British official historians were condemnatory in their criticism of Wilson who they claimed 'lost touch with the realities of war'.[64] The poor planning by Clark, 'perhaps the most egocentric Allied general of the War', and Alexander, who 'acquired a false reputation as a great commander in the field', along with Freyberg's mistakes meant that the German defence strategy worked better than it should have done given the overpowering numbers.[65] It has been claimed by one historian that 'on the whole both 5th and 8th Armies were poorly led during the Cassino battles, where operations were consistently marred by lack of strategic vision and slipshod staff work'.[66]

Given this survey of postwar criticism it is apparent that there were serious blunders in the Allied leadership; clearly the strong German defence had caused deep frustration for the Allied commanders, who at this stage and despite having overwhelming resources and logistics on their side, could not break through the Gustav Line at Cassino for the Liri valley, nor could they break out of the landing beach at Nettuno. In his own observations von Senger wrote that 'we could not see any military reason for choosing this moment for its destruction, for although a few single attacks were to follow, the main battle had already petered out'.[67] It was curious that von Senger singled out his query on the attack by arguing that the battle had 'petered out'. He must have known that given the resources of his enemies that it had not quietened down, but a pause caused by probably considering how to break through or circumnavigate the area. The German control of the Cassino heights, to within a few metres and more probably within the shadows of the Abbey's tall walls meant that for infantry to climb to the attack was all but a suicide action, and although some argued that circumnavigating may have been the better option, bombing may well have been under discussion. The battle had paused but not petered out.

Von Senger also noted that Kesselring had wanted the monastery 'neutralised' and had ordered von Senger to protect some ancient bishoprics and the art and relics of the monastery. In his postwar interrogation and trial, Kesselring found Italian support for his assisting the Church and helping to try and preserve its ancient structures. It was apparent that Kesselring 'was, of course, perfectly aware of the need to protect buildings and works of art' and this has been acknowledged in *The Rape of Europa*, a study devoted to finding and returning stolen treasures.[68] 'Considering the precarious position of the German Armies north of Naples, it was an extraordinary use of military effort', and given the general impression of German attitudes was something of a surprise, when following the Allied destruction of Monte Cassino a number of reputable Italians came to Kesselring's support.[69] Elsewhere the Germany military had paid little respect to Church property and life. There is little doubt that von Senger was in full support of Kesselring (who was himself Roman Catholic) in his efforts not to destroy Italy's heritage and its Catholic foundations.*

Kesselring, like von Senger, was an educated man who appreciated Italy's culture, unlike the infamous Göring who was plundering art throughout Europe. A Lieutenant Colonel Schlegel, who 'before the war had been an art historian and librarian', was the true instigator behind saving the considerable treasures at Monte Cassino, and is still honoured there to this day.[70] When this Schlegel and a Lieutenant Becker, members of the Herman Göring Division approached the Abbot, Dom Gregorio Diamare, suggesting they save the treasures and library, the monks were suspicious because of Göring's reputation as 'perhaps the most celebrated snapper-up of unconsidered trifles in the Second World War.'[71] Eventually they accepted this once Ernst Weizsäcker spoke with Kesselring, who, with von Senger, authorised they be transported to the Vatican, hopefully a safer place. After the war Kesselring implied that he was the true saviour of the Cassino treasures; he may well have signed the order, but the initiative started with men like von Senger and especially Schlegel. Despite Schlegel's SS background, von Senger found him honest and prepared to help. In a report written on 3 May 1946 by the Chief of Staff of XIV *Panzerkorps*, Oster, he recorded how there had been serious doubts about Göring's intentions regarding the works of art and the way von Senger had taken control. Von Senger also worked hard to protect the neutrality of the convent buildings. He also added that von Senger had been instructed to ignore giving aid to the convents which von Senger completely ignored.[72]

Most of the art treasures of Naples had been placed in the monastery for safe-keeping, and 'considering the precarious position of the German

* Until the German Ambassador Dr Rahn's memoirs were published few knew of Hitler's intention to have the Vatican 'fumigated' by German troops, see Westphal, *The German Army in the West* (London: Cassell, 1951), p.168. It was considered that the Pope should be imprisoned, and the Vatican robbed of its priceless treasures, see Dan Kurzman, *A Special Mission* (New York: Da Capo Press, 2007).

armies north of Naples, it was an extraordinary use of military effort'.[73] It was suspected with some justification that not all the work arrived at the Vatican but an appeal 'was made to Kesselring himself ... the recalcitrant Göring Division finally agreed to return part of their holdings'.[74] Some Italian treasures were purloined and some lost forever, but even Kesselring's most ardent critics acknowledged that this was not his doing. According to von Weizsäcker, German ambassador to the Vatican, Rome's survival was due to the Pope and Kesselring, von Senger is not mentioned but there is no question he was also one of the key figures in these efforts.[75]

Von Senger with Kesselring's backup had ensured that the military would not make use of the Abbey as a military outpost, though they knew its height was invaluable for observation. Von Senger admitted that halfway up the hill, but not in the Abbey they had concealed observers' posts. However, it was probably more than halfway, and today it is known they were within a few hundred yards, and it is inconceivable that they were not armed. Von Senger had also assumed that the Allies must have known that the Abbey had been neutralised by the Germans as the Vatican were well aware of the situation, and they knew that civilians from the town had therefore sought refuge in the Abbey.

More to the point, von Senger wrote that the bombing of the Abbey meant they could inhabit the ruins with weapons which in the rubble could be more easily concealed, while in the town there was little chance of the dreaded tanks making their way through the destruction. The bombing in his view had helped the defence by blocking the way for the attackers. The 82-year-old Abbot, according to von Senger, led with a processional crucifix a group of survivors of monks and refugees, but being continually in danger of shell fire, so a safer route was organised, and the Abbot was brought to von Senger's headquarters at Castel Massimo where he spent the night. The next day he found himself in an embarrassing situation as the OKW wanted the Abbot interviewed by radio reporting on the behaviour of German troops. He did not want the Abbot to be placed in such an uncomfortable situation, but he thought that the proposed propaganda was for once good. It had been von Senger's aim to move the Abbot to the central Benedictine monastery at Saint Anselmo where the current Abbot was Baron Stotzingen who came from the same area as von Senger, and they had been friends from earlier days. Instead, the Abbot's car was ordered elsewhere for more radio broadcasts thereby becoming an unwilling tool in the political conflict, even though all he had to say was true. Goebbels and Ribbentrop also demanded he had to be taken to the German Embassy in the Vatican, where he was asked 'to sign a memorandum that bristled with propaganda against the Allies', but the Abbot refused to sign the document.[76] The truth was evident to everyone, the Abbot did not have to point out that the Allies had destroyed the ancient Christian edifice, but he was not going to be a protagonist and take sides. Von Senger protested about all this to Kesselring who simply replied there was nothing he could do about the situation.

Amazingly, von Senger then turned in his memoirs to understanding Allied motives and reasons, involving himself in the debate over the bombing, criticising those who attacked Mark Clark for authorising the bombing. He asked whether the New Zealanders would expect their sons to die for the sake of an ancient building, taking up a point once made by Field Marshal Alexander that it was wrong to lose men for the sake of an old building. The only error which von Senger took up was that storming the heights should have happened at once and not be delayed for a couple of days, a point which for many contained much truth. Von Senger pointed out that for the ordinary soldier it would have been surprising to learn that the Germans were not using the Abbey. Von Senger thought it was an idle waste to criticise the enemy's tactics in the fighting but admits there were military tactical failures on the Allied side. This was probably a postwar additional thought as von Senger was very much engaged in healing the wounds created by the conflict. He pointed out that in German military theory one does not slacken the battle even after bombing. Such was the horrendous and devastating bombing he was probably right that an immediate attack may well have worked, but from ground level it is also easy to understand that after watching such a bombing raid it could be assumed that few survived. Von Senger knew from his experience in First World War trench warfare that shelling could look just as destructive, but survivors still emerged to fight. He knew that in the Abbey destruction only clergy and civilians died, not one German, but then he had inside knowledge. In his postwar analysis he appears much more understanding and placatory than one might expect. It raises two questions; did he have the same empathy with the allies in 1944 or, as mentioned, was it part of his character to try and heal wounds?

He recalled at the time his main concern was 'an attack by Juin's corps with its superb Moroccan and Algerian divisions'.[77] Most commentators then and since have often noted the brutal and ruthless approach of the French Colonial troops, but part of von Senger's placatory nature was to describe them as 'superb'. As a battlefield general von Senger always had deep respect for the French forces, it was von Senger who had warned Kesselring that they were endangering the Cassino defence, causing Kesselring to milk his reserves for assistance.[78] The Moroccans were known as the Goumiers, they had a fearful reputation, feared by the Italians in North Africa and the Germans in Italy, and there are many instances of their barbaric behaviour, but when it came to winning wars von Senger was right to describe them as superb fighters, and when it came to moral conduct von Senger by this stage would have known about the criminal and immoral orders carried out by Himmler's SS and even some Wehrmacht.

While writing his account of the bitter battles for Cassino, von Senger found time to write about a comrade called General Ernst-Günther Baade who at Cassino was the commander of 90 Panzer Grenadier Division, well-known for its fighting ability, and who had played a major part in averting defeat at the first Cassino battle. On the very last day of the war while on the way home he died in an air attack, and von Senger wrote a memorial for Baade for the journal of Cavalry Regiment 3. It was clear that for von Senger, who had known Baade for some time, not least when he had helped organise with a degree of brilliance the escape from Sicily of German and Italian troops, that he helped save the day in the initial battle for Cassino. He described his background, not least his international showjumping along with his wife, but mainly because of his leadership qualities and some eccentric behaviour. Von Senger gave this unconventional officer 'plenty of rein' because he admired his qualities, which is worth mentioning because it demonstrates what von Senger valued in good officers. Baade influenced his troops by being with them right up in the front line. He mentioned the time that when in North Africa he and some men had broken into British lines, and he used a captured officer to guide them through the minefield, which when done as an act of gratitude set the British officer free again to return to his post. On one occasion the OKW had asked von Senger whether it was true Baade had dined with the enemy, which was nonsense, but von Senger was aware that by using radio he had exchanged Christmas wishes with the enemy. He often dressed in a Scottish khaki kilt over his normal battledress, but in place of the sporran he carried a large pistol. He always made a point of digging in at the frontline which von Senger found dangerous when he wanted to find him. He was with Baade when the Abbey was annihilated, and it was his troops which stopped the New Zealand Corps making further advances. Being ex-cavalry, he was a man who understood the need for mobility on the battlefield. This sudden act of a few memorial pages to this unusual Commander is useful in understanding von Senger's character because he was writing about a man who was brave, understood the importance of mobile tactics, cared for his men, and influenced them in the best way. He was not the traditional image of a senior German officer, and it is easy to read between the lines that von Senger admired these qualities which he hoped reflected himself, possibly hoping that one day someone would see him in the same light.

The Second Battle of Cassino

As mentioned above the bombing raid which destroyed the Abbey started again on 15 March, which von Senger found as perplexing as the first, and for which both sides had its critics. The second bombing raid caused a considerable amount of what is now dubbed 'blue on blue' damage, not helped by bomb aiming devices being somewhat limited in a confusing landscape of valleys and high terrain. Von Senger noted that the first bombing had given no operational advantage to the enemy, so this was directed at German troops. In his postwar analysis he was quick to note the political problems, not least the New Zealand demand that their commander Freyberg had a governmental demand that if he thought an attack would lead to a thousand deaths of his men, he had the right to veto the plan, but was reluctant to apply this emergency button. When he had a conversation with Field Marshal Alexander and was told another division would be detailed, he decided to carry on. Von Senger even looked again at the wider implications of the worrying

Russian progress in a war which the Germans could not win. It would be interesting to know if this were in his mind in 1944 or postwar, and it is tempting, given his intellectual strength and political views, to give him the benefit of any doubt. It is clear from his memoirs that he had read the various postwar accounts and historical findings which were beginning to emerge in the 1950s.

Generally, he realised that the second bombing had not assisted the Allies as much as they hoped, because it had caused them damage, and created yet more rubble making it impossible for their armour to make any real progress. He also noted that many ordinary Italian houses had arched cellars where civilians and soldiers could take shelter. The fighting reflected the battle for Stalingrad, close encounters, house by house, and not knowing if the enemy were in the same building but on a different floor, which made it difficult to know whether to use artillery. There were hidden batteries, and von Senger described the difficulty of moving around the area as he often tried, like his friend Baade, to stay in touch with those at the front line. He had fought in Russia to relieve Stalingrad but not in the city, and the encounter at Cassino reminded him more of the close combat fighting in the trench war of 1914–18. It was also difficult, understandably, for him as a commander to have a clear picture of what was happening.

At this stage his troops were under attack by the New Zealanders and the 4th Indian Division, who were coming from a southerly direction towards the monastery hill. He thought highly of the attacking troops but could see their climbing and crossing of steep gradients made the attack extremely dangerous. He noted they could not use their tanks because of the rubble, and one day they were hit by a heavy rainstorm turning the debris and earth into a thick quagmire, making movement difficult if not impossible. He also found that his side's use of smoke-making shells added to the confusion of those attacking. He noted a general reluctance by the enemy to throw in reserves at places where German tactics would have deemed it essential. It could be argued that although the German tactics may have been better, Allied commanders were understandably more reticent to lose their men's lives. The better side of human nature emerged, according to von Senger, when in the close combat areas, a strange intimacy developed between the fighting opponents when they accepted that the other side could send out medics unharmed to help the wounded. Agreements with time limits were accepted when the medics could go out in the exposed terrain to help those wounded. This was the better side of human nature which von Senger noted with a sense of relief.

On 19 March, such was the stubbornness of the defenders in this yard by yard fighting that Freyberg had to send in reserves which had been held back in anticipation of pursuing the enemy after the hoped-for breakthrough. The localised battle had reached a position of virtual stalemate, which had typified the Cassino conflicts from the time they started. In one of the earlier books studying the Cassino battles, written in 1957 by Fred Majdalany and read by von Senger, the author noted the details. He had observed that von Senger's defence lines had worked, and even as Clark's 5th Army attacked 'von Senger was able to plug the holes as they appeared', pointing out von Senger was an Anglophile and 'an officer whose known anti-Nazi feelings resulted in his contribution to the defence of Cassino being played down by the German authorities'.[79]

When von Senger reached this point in his memoirs he continued down his traditional literary route of pausing to reflect on the battle in retrospect. He noted that internationally the Cassino battle was of interest because of the stubborn German defence and lack of progress by the Allies, as if they had come up against a brick wall. After three months' fighting the Allies had only made in the region of 15 kilometres. The German propaganda machine was making the most of what was happening, first the destruction of the ancient monastery, and now the stubborn German defence and the Allied lack of progress. Despite holding some high positions, von Senger noted their main problem was being constantly taken by surprise, as their reconnaissance was not that good, and every time the enemy attacked it came as a surprise. The Luftwaffe had lost any hold in the area and could not be used to spot what was happening at ground level. There were few prisoners of any value to interrogate, and it was impossible for agents to pass though the line even by using sea-routes. On the other hand, the enemy had complete control of the skies which was good for observation purposes and therefore for counterattack, though the front line at this stage remained fairly static. Von Senger was astute enough to know the situation could not remain stable, especially if the enemy decided to become more mobile.

For his personal work he controlled the operations in all sectors and used his knowledge of the terrain to the best of his ability, changing units when appropriate. He made a point of paying constant attention to the morale of his troops, and he would often be seen working his way from one sector to another. This he knew was the German tradition of ensuring the men under his command knew he cared for them, believing that the German traditions were the best in the world. He was correct in so far that in Germany, led by Prussian traditions, the military was given the highest social status and great pride was taken in its professional approach. He even reflected on one occasion when he met Field Marshal Sir John Dill, later the Chief of the Imperial Staff on manoeuvres in East Prussian in 1935, who had been curious about German methods.

However, his pleasure in writing about the old German military was realistically levelled to the situation when the Second World War started. Under Hitler the situation had changed drastically, and he mentioned commanders now sheltering under the directives issued by Hitler, so individual commanders, unlike in the past, could not make their own judgements but had to wait on OKW, or in other words, Hitler's orders. If there were any singular turning point in this war it was probably the battle of Stalingrad, where General Paulus and nearly all the German military commanders in Russia knew the only hope was to break out of the Stalingrad encirclement while they could. Instead, Hitler issued his well-worn command of stand and fight, which was not only a serious military misjudgement, but showed no care for his officers and soldiers. Despite these facts, von Senger, although blaming Hitler, saw the causes of German failure as running deeper. He believed the art of communications had not helped. Unlike previous wars he noted that in the Second World War it was possible to speak to senior commanders in a matter of minutes, which placed the responsibility of direction further up the chain, and away from the commander on the frontline. As a consequence of this development von Senger felt many frontline commanders were becoming more and more dependent on orders from higher command issued through wireless or telephone messages. If the local commander ignored this new development, he knew he could be in serious trouble. This was not just a German issue, and one well-known British general once said that the Duke of Wellington was lucky not to have a telephone system.

In terms of tactics von Senger then wrote about holding the line when different units fought side by side, and it was essential they communicated with one another in order to keep the front line stable, otherwise a decision to withdraw by one commander may leave a serious and unprepared dent in the line. It was this danger which meant that in von Senger's opinion a council of war was essential. Von Senger commented on the North African war which in the popular mind involved vast spaces, but in reality, mobility was limited by the sea on one side and a vast desert on the other, which meant a narrow front resulting in sudden attacks or withdrawals.

These two factors accounted for the reduction of the independence of field commanders, with the third factor the diminishing number of forces. Von Senger believed that with the modern developments there was a lack of infantry men which he suffered from in Cassino, leaving a lack of essential reserves. This made it essential that when there was a lack of reserves, they should be kept under the eye of the army group and allocated when and where necessary, which again was essential in his work at Cassino. Von Senger pointed out that the OKW had formulated the policy of emergency units for such occasions, but in Von Senger's opinion thy never had any real fighting value. Infantry men could not be replaced by artillery or communication troops.

Amongst the major problems the forces at Cassino suffered from occurred when the critical bridges crossing deep ravines and huge rivers had been destroyed by aircraft. The Allies ruled the airways, which often halted any supply routes, and the Luftwaffe was unable to drop supplies. If repairs were attempted, they became the immediate focus of attack. The enemy air superiority also meant that any form of troop movement was easily spotted, which meant only movement at night was possible. The commanders in these situations had to learn to adapt quickly as circumstances changed. The main issue for von Senger remained the hopelessness of the Nazi development of waiting orders from the top. This led to a clash of thoughts in von Senger's own thinking as he often promulgated that the commander must see for himself what is happening and ensure his presence bolstered the morale of the fighting troops. On the other hand, if he were not at his headquarters, he missed the opportunity to influence what was happening elsewhere in his chain of command, having to leave it with his chief-of-staff. Von Senger admitted he was often away from his central headquarters while visiting the frontline, as he had admired General Baade for the same habit. He concluded by writing that 'in Hitler's army there was no satisfaction in being a commander'.[80] He wondered how history would judge those who knew in all honesty that the war was lost and yet continued to fight and shed blood. In Stalingrad General Paulus knew the war was lost and fought on, and it may be that von Senger, with his religious feelings may have paused and wondered about fighting for an immoral regime. He concluded his analysis by dwelling on the fact that his headquarters were in Roccasecca, where St. Thomas Aquinas was born in 1225, noting that to that moment in time 'his teachings are still basically relevant to Western morality. They stipulate that no man can be held answerable for the misdeeds of those over whom he has no power'.[81] This sentence in his memoirs almost gives the impression that von Senger was desperately trying to find some theological reason for his own salvation, even though he was serving a dictator whom he knew to be criminal and immoral.

In his next step reflecting on the Cassino battles he turned his attention to the use of infantry, which he described as the 'Queen of the Battlefield'. Because of the nature of the Cassino battles von Senger spent time on the nature of infantry as this was the main strength of the German defence. He described that the battle was not a long single line as in a trench type warfare, but a series of strong points watching and guarding specific areas. In daylight hours it was virtually impossible to view or communicate from one point to another, but this had to be done under cover of darkness. He was also working with reduced numbers, and compared with the Great War there were fewer men keeping any eye on the greater distances, which would have been too risky in the Great War. To keep the front steady under these circumstances, von Senger ordered that a second line was built in so that they could replace casualties as soon as possible. It was the second line which had to be added to in case of an emergency, which von Senger described as a 'rallying force'. Despite the problems of numbers von Senger noted that his troops still held firm. He would often see them fighting to maintain their position within some 'blockhouse' or for maintaining their presence on some high craggy outcrop of rock. He deliberately kept the groups in smaller numbers to avoid too much attrition and hold the capability of sending in fresh numbers.

He made some interesting observations about the atmosphere of his war zone in the mountains. It was, he pointed out, almost impossible to hold conversations at times because of the noise of exploding shells and bombs in rocky valleys, where the noise was not only magnified, but tended to echo and re-echo in prolonged waves. It proved impossible to use the supply routes and it took time to cover even a kilometre, as even at night the enemy could infiltrate these tracks. It was not helped by the knowledge that the enemy knew the Germans could not raise counterattacks and could only defend, which gave the enemy time to build up its own strength. He painted a picture of a hopeless situation for the frontline soldiers, desperately holding onto positions against larger numbers who were better equipped, and knowing they were in the constant danger of a breakout from Anzio beach behind them. Many on the Allied side, including Field Marshal Alexander, had been amazed at their fighting abilities and courage. Using a rocky landscape the Germans were holding a jagged line across a dangerous terrain holding back massive forces. In his memoirs von Senger even took time to list the names of some of his men. After the battle he spoke on German radio about their bravery over such a fraught lengthy time. Von Senger reminded his listeners that they were not fighting in pleasant sunny climes, but that the mountains and hills where the battle took place had the harshest weather often with freezing snowstorms endangering life. Because of the landscape it was impossible to dig into the rocky ground for cover, and he gave full credit to General Baade and others, not once trying to bring any credit onto his own efforts, and even in his memoirs it is necessary to read them carefully and deduce his own bravery. Instead, as in the radio broadcast, he always mentioned other names from senior officers to the ordinary soldiers.

He was right to mention the weather and terrain because the battles around the Cassino sector amounted to mountain warfare. Even the high hills in the Abruzzi region would be considered mountains by most visitors and would be taken seriously by mountain soldiers such as the well-known Alpine troops. Von Senger also raised the problem that much of the fighting and movement took place at night, noting that Russians with their long dark winters were accustomed to this, but not those in Western Europe. Von Senger noted that the only mountain troops which

Fridolin Rudolph von Senger und Etterlin.

In France von Senger, like many others, was amazed at the speed of victory, May 1940. (*Bundesarchiv Picture 146-1978-062-24, photograph by Schmidt*)

The dreaded T-34 Russian tank during the Battle of Moscow, December 1941.

His habit of chatting to soldiers, this time an Italian soldier in Sicily, summer 1943. (*Bundesarchiv Picture 1011-305-0651-26, photograph by Schmidt Focher Hauke*)

In Sicily cheerful Italian soldiers surrender – many never wanted the war, July–August 1943. (*National Museum of the U.S. Navy, LC-USZ62-98976*)

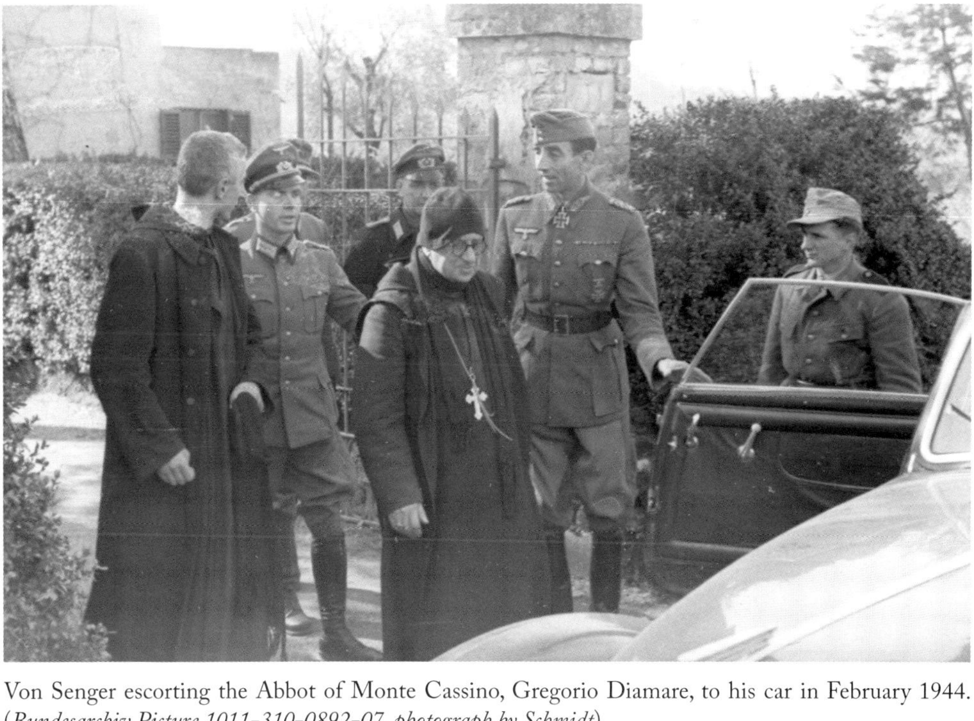

Von Senger escorting the Abbot of Monte Cassino, Gregorio Diamare, to his car in February 1944. (*Bundesarchiv Picture 1011-310-0892-07, photograph by Schmidt*)

Von Senger's 'hawk-like' smile.

Von Senger's tall, athletic build, pictured here in March 1944. (*Bundesarchiv Picture 101I-311-0914-10A*)

Working with Kesselring on battle plans. Notice the characteristic vein on his forehead.

Discussions on the battlefield.

As the last commander of troops in Italy, von Senger is seen here in conversation with Generals Douglas Packard and Donald Brann to discuss terms of the German surrender.

Meeting General Clark to discuss terms of surrender. (*IWM NA 24791, photographer Sergeant Bowman, No. 2 Army Film and Photographic Unit*)

Discussing surrender terms, 4 May 1945. (*USA Signal Corps Archives, photographer S/Sgt S. Elson, 196th Signal Photo Co.*)

General Clark handing von Senger the terms of surrender.

His friend General Dostler before his execution, 1 December 1945. Von Senger stood as a witness at his trial. (*NARA*)

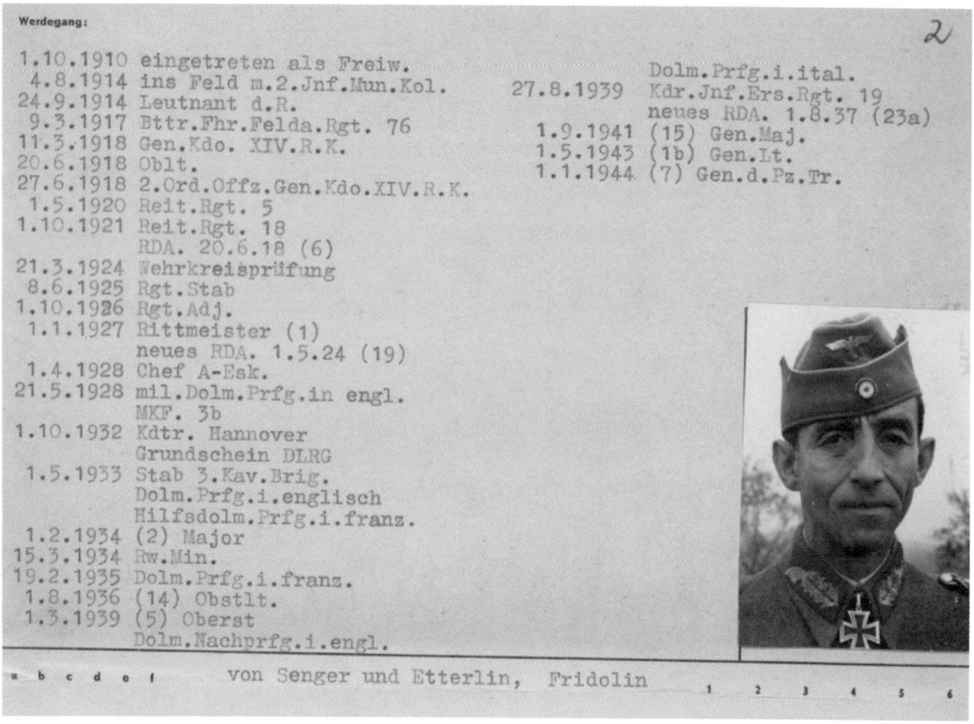

Werdegang: 2

1.10.1910 eingetreten als Freiw.
4.8.1914 ins Feld m.2.Jnf.Mun.Kol.
24.9.1914 Leutnant d.R.
9.3.1917 Bttr.Fhr.Felda.Rgt. 76
11.3.1918 Gen.Kdo. XIV.R.K.
20.6.1918 Oblt.
27.6.1918 2.Ord.Offz.Gen.Kdo.XIV.R.K.
1.5.1920 Reit.Rgt. 5
1.10.1921 Reit.Rgt. 18
RDA. 20.6.18 (6)
21.3.1924 Wehrkreisprüfung
8.6.1925 Rgt.Stab
1.10.1926 Rgt.Adj.
1.1.1927 Rittmeister (1)
neues RDA. 1.5.24 (19)
1.4.1928 Chef A-Esk.
21.5.1928 mil.Dolm.Prfg.in engl.
MKF. 3b
1.10.1932 Kdtr. Hannover
Grundschein DLRG
1.5.1933 Stab 3.Kav.Brig.
Dolm.Prfg.i.englisch
Hilfsdolm.Prfg.i.franz.
1.2.1934 (2) Major
15.3.1934 Rw.Min.
19.2.1935 Dolm.Prfg.i.franz.
1.8.1936 (14) Obstlt.
1.3.1939 (5) Oberst
Dolm.Nachprfg.i.engl.
Dolm.Prfg.i.ital.
27.8.1939 Kdr.Jnf.Ers.Rgt. 19
neues RDA. 1.8.37 (23a)
1.9.1941 (15) Gen.Maj.
1.5.1943 (1b) Gen.Lt.
1.1.1944 (7) Gen.d.Pz.Tr.

a b c d e f von Senger und Etterlin, Fridolin 1 2 3 4 5 6

Von Senger's military record from German archives.

Von Senger in the BBC Face to Face interview, 1959.

were eventually sent to Cassino were Austrian who 'suffered from a severe moral strain', and who in reality knew little about hard mountain warfare having been trained in hills, some of their field postcards stating they 'would rather return to Russia on all fours'.[82] Eventually von Senger noted that these troops did rise to the occasion and proved good opponents even against the French Colonial troops from mountain regions.

Getting supplies to the defence outpost was difficult and they had to use mules, a task these soldiers knew little about and had to learn quickly. The foods tended to be typical military powder, but von Senger noted they had to be full of the necessary nutrients which they had to prepare while being on duty with constant alertness. Another issue these hard-pressed soldiers had to face was the dangerous task of evacuating the wounded as a stretcher demanded four men, and to assist this problem von Senger suggested seat barrows, apparently used in skiing. They also designated hidden areas where they could hide ammunition stocks to save the danger of too many long hauls, but shortages remained an ongoing problem. Curiously von Senger noted that the Allies used helicopters for surveillance. Helicopters were in their infancy of use in 1944, and they would have been rare to see. It was the air dominance which the Germans could not match which created many of the problems for the defenders both in their positions and their movements. Nevertheless, against a force of much greater numbers and diverse weaponry, it indicated the German infantry put up an astounding defence. Numerically it is not ascertainable the numbers involved, which differed from one skirmish to another, but it was clear that a few determined men used the terrain to hold back vastly superior forces.

The stand-off, as it was not a stalemate, gave von Senger some free time. His headquarters belonged to an Italian the Marchese Campanari who lived nearby. He had once been an Italian cavalry officer who did not want the humiliation of being disarmed by the Germans, and he had dressed as a cattle drover to make his way home. He was not alien towards the Germans and von Senger took him under his protection, and he would dine with him, his wife and daughter; it appeared to be a genuine friendship which continued postwar. He would also dine with the Benedictine nuns who were probably astounded to find a German general who was a Lay Benedictine. He also knew a Bishop Baroncelli in nearby Veroli. This Bishop had been ordained to this post in Veroli only the year before and would hold several bishoprics in Italy until his death in 1972. When there was a prolonged silence on the battlefield, von Senger even managed to visit Rome. He could hear distant gunfire coming from the Anzio beachhead area, but he managed to view the sites of the city he loved, especially some of his old haunts. Again, he met the Chief Abbot, Baron Stotzingen and received the host from his own hands at High Mass, afterwards lunching together.

He discovered speaking to his friends that the defence of Cassino had succeeded in regaining the impression amongst the Italian civilians of stabilising German-Italian relationships as German invincibility seemed to be returning. This was at least what his friends told him, but Italy remained in turmoil politically. Technically it now had two governments as Mussolini had been rescued and was head of Hitler's puppet government, although local to Salo still had some wide fascist support. Most Italians only wanted the war to end, but there were also many prepared to fight against the Germans which emerged in the bitter partisan war. Although south of Cassino, Italy was in Allied hands, many found the living conditions difficult under foreign rule with a serious shortage of food, and there were reports that living under British and American rule was often quite tough. Von Senger also heard that many in Naples were living off prostitution, which was a rumour with truth, as it is now known that venereal diseases in that area had become widespread and serious. Naples was developing an appalling reputation and had become the base for 'I & I', Intercourse and Intoxication, and was not only full of this disease but unbelievably corrupt. A virulent strain of typhus had raged through the city and although it was hushed up for many years, over a million Neapolitans had to be sprayed with DDT. Even the prevalent venereal disease was 70 per cent resistant to sulpha, which was then the understood cure. It was estimated that 60 per cent of the women suffered from this disease, and one out of every ten soldiers suffered the problem: at one time it appeared that 15 per cent of all hospital beds had VD patients. Another frightening statistic showed that two-thirds of the economic growth of Naples depended on stolen American goods; it was as if for every five ships arriving in port one disappeared every time. On one occasion an entire trainload of sugar disappeared, and it was said that if one yawned your gold teeth would disappear.[83] In Naples the French Colonial troops committed over 100 murders and over 3,000 rapes, and in a biography, Captain Robert Maxwell revealed he shot unarmed German civilians.[84] It was understandable given the mayhem that Italians remained politically divided between fascism and democracy, and between Germans and the Allies. Adding to this confusion were the upper crust monarchists, the Church, the nobility, and those who had nothing to lose.

Von Senger expressed a degree of compassion for women caught up on this conflict, especially when ordered to evacuate their homes with their children, protesting that they would starve and would rather be blown up by a shell. Von Senger put up what he described as a 'passive resistance' to evacuation, but the numbers fleeing north would simply be following the war as it too moved north. It was not surprising that the Italian harvests had little to offer in a country occupied by various nationalities and with the population at starvation level. Von Senger noted the Italian families of the old Papal State were more friendly to the Germans, not least because there were many blood-ties, and even though the Nazi regime had rejected catholic and other denominations, this did not seem to disturb this warmer relationship. This was probably because they knew that von Senger, a German general had retained his loyalty to the Catholic Church. Von Senger felt at this moment he was leading a double life, enjoying friendship, comfort, and his surroundings, all in the midst of a bitter war.

On 17 April he handed over the command of his XIV Panzer Corps to a deputy he did not name. He had been instructed to make his way to the Führer Headquarters to receive a decoration. He felt reluctant to leave his staff, many of whom had become good friends, and had a sense that times were changing for him. He enjoyed the ride north towards Ravenna, a place where he felt times had not changed for twelve centuries. His love of history was evident, and he rightly saw Ravenna as the old place where west met east. He spent time adoring views of the city, and he does not mention the rest of the trip to Hitler's Headquarters. In terms of the ceremony his cynicism returned noting that 'everyone now had these awards and decorations', and as such it lacked any personal significance. There were many there for these awards and von Senger found it 'impressive in a rather negative' way, wondering how many of the younger officers would react. He was aware that although he regarded Hitler with extreme distaste, he was stunned by the way so many Germans still supported a man with such a nihilistic will and knowing that many of the younger officers still saw the Führer as a demi-god. He described Hitler's dress as unbecoming for the occasion as he was wearing a yellow military blouse, a yellow tie, but with a white collar and black trousers. His description almost fits the imagination of someone describing a clown. Hitler's size and short neck offered no sense of dignity, and von Senger described his complexion as looking flabby and his famous blue eyes appeared watery. His handshake was weak, his left arm limp, and trembling, and unlike the image of a shouting dictator his quiet voice almost, unbelievably, aroused a sense of compassion in von Senger as it seemed to expose the man's despondency and weakness. Despite this last piece of the description which von Senger modifies with 'almost', it is apparent from his extensive description of the Führer his detestation of the man was abundantly clear. Even Hitler's conversation was depressing, mentioning the Eastern Front which had become a series of defeats, that the Battle of the Atlantic was proving difficult because of Allied radar, and he never mentioned Italy which Goebbels had been exploiting. For the more astute Hitler would have appeared behind his own times as 1943, the year before this meeting, the Eastern Front was collapsing before the Soviet onslaught, and at sea it was more dangerous to be on a U-boat than in a convoy. Italy had been used by Goebbels because of the German defence both at Cassino and locking the beachhead at Anzio, but most would have known that it would eventually break. Hitler expressed concern that the likelihood of an invasion by the Allies on mainland Europe was becoming more likely. Von Senger noted the whole meeting was depressing, and that there was no mention of the secret weapons on which the German public had become reliant. Von Senger wondered if the younger officers felt the same, concluding they had been fed too long on Nazi propaganda. General Baade was there and shared the same opinion as von Senger.

Having received his award von Senger had to attend a course on *Weltanschauung* (World View) at the castle of Sonthofen. Hundreds attended and had anticipated Hitler would appear on the final day, but to the disappointment of many this did not happen. Von Senger described

Keitel's optimistic speeches which von Senger knew had no ground, as 'Himmler's artificial joviality'. Von Senger spotted that even senior officers from the OKW did not appear enthusiastic. The interesting line which von Senger adds was that a 'fear of a revolution had made the die-hard followers of Hitler keep an eye on [politically] unreliable generals', with von Senger observing that he was often treated with some reserve.[85] For many it would have been no surprise that von Senger was there to be indoctrinated, he had made no secret of his views, and it was probably only because of his soldierly conduct in Italy, often known as the 'backwater' war, that he was to remain safe.

Von Senger wondered what would happen, concerned that it was not just a matter of Germany ridding itself of Hitler, but the need to finish off the entire Nazi machine. He was aware that some thought that with Hitler dead the Allies might open negotiations, but von Senger realised that many foreigners would blame German militarism which had helped Hitler to power and gave him the tools for war. Even in the resistance which planned Hitler's assassination there were some willing to go ahead but knowing it was for Germany's enemies too late in the day, and unconditional surrender had already been an Allied pronouncement. After this course Von Senger was granted some leave, but on 12 May heard that the offensive in Italy had started again, and it was not until 17 May he returned to the front.

The Allied Breakthrough in Italy

When he returned von Senger found his headquarters occupied by the Commander-in-Chief of the 10th Army as their own HQ had been bombed. He had heard that at the Anzio beachhead, which he always referred to as Nettuno, the German 14th Army had failed to make progress against the Allies. He had a private conversation with Kesselring who told him the fighting spirit of the forces had lacked a degree of determination, and they were hampered by the naval guns against which they could do nothing. This perplexing problem was not helped, yet again, by the terrain which was not suitable for the use of tanks. This had all raised the question as to the sense of trying to maintain two army fronts, north and south of Cassino.

Historically the Anzio beachhead had been a serious problem for both sides since it had first taken place on 22 January. The landing, as mentioned above, was successful in terms of putting huge numbers of men and equipment ashore, but Kesselring's rapid reaction had trapped Churchill's 'stranded whale' on the beach. At Anzio Kesselring recalled the Allies being cautious in the Great War, as well as Montgomery's failure to break through following his success at the Sangro, and saw this as the same element of caution.[86] General Lucas was initially supported in his cautious approach of staying put by Clark and Alexander, who, recalling the near failure of Salerno, suggested the need to build-up forces; Maitland Wilson called this the 'Salerno complex'. On the Allied side there has always been a long debate as to the delay of striking inland with General Lucas shouldering much of the blame. The situation stalemated, and as German numbers increased both Allied Commanders and Churchill criticised the hapless Lucas. Some have argued the distance between Rome and Anzio was too great to defend, and Lucas had been made the scapegoat. Lucas found support in the memoirs of Major General Harmon and Major General Temple who pointed out that 'the Germans produced seven Divisions in ten days with plenty of armour'.[87] Kesselring had lacked aerial reconnaissance, and had not been helped by Admiral Canaris who had issued a categorical denial of a planned invasion, and who had just taken to the air when the invasion started.[88] The policeman Schellenberg suspected Canaris of treachery, and Kesselring's ignorance of the impending invasion meant he had sent reserves to the southern front leaving Rome exposed.[89] Canaris was later executed for being part of the resistance against Hitler and his regime. It was because of Canaris' misinformation that Kesselring had promised to send von Senger two divisions.

Although there were some 50,000 Allied troops ashore, the situation was static as they were hemmed in, as Lucas ordered more digging in while the Germans increased their encirclement. At the end of January, General Lucas had attempted the first tentative breakout from Anzio, around Cisterna and Campoleone. Edward Grace, a Gordon Highlanders' officer, referred to this area as the bitterest fighting of the war, and more akin to the trenches of the Great War.[90] For Kesselring it was a matter of anticipating the next move; he had reliable commanders such as General

Richard Heidrich in charge of paratroopers, and von Senger's friend General Baade who constantly secured the area.

At a critical stage Hitler interfered, ordering that the Infantry Demonstration (*Lehr*) Regiment be sent for the assault. As Kesselring noted, this was a home-defence force with no battle exposure. They not only lacked experience, but because of the timing of the planned attack, it meant they would be fighting in unfamiliar terrain in the dark. Hitler's interference cost 3,000 men and thirty tanks: Kesselring wrote 'they were thrown back disgracefully'.[91] By 1 March Kesselring realised the Germans would fail simply because of the sheer number of Allied tanks. They had failed for two reasons: the first was the sheer size of the Allied reserves and naval support, but secondly Hitler's inane interference, having insisted the wrong regiment lead the assault, and Kesselring could not challenge him.

Lucas was eventually replaced by Truscott, with orders to breakout from the bridgehead. By 11 March there were some 90,000 Americans and 35,000 British ashore. Kesselring expressed the obvious concern that the Allied commanders were becoming battle-experienced and producing better combat formations, and in an interesting insight Kesselring criticised German propaganda for goading the Allies for lack of initiative.[92] Kesselring ordered the strengthening of parts of the Gustav Line to enable defensive retreats, and also strengthened the switch-lines to the Hitler Line, renamed the von Senger Bolt Line, mainly because Hitler did not want his name associated with potential failure, and it was von Senger who was holding that area. The Anzio beachhead still seemed frozen and 'Kesselring used this hiatus to create a new defensive line, the Caesar C Line, to contain the beachhead'.[93] Kesselring was professional in his approach, as were his subordinates, and in reality the Allied command was inexperienced.

As von Senger was appraised of the emerging dangers in mid-May, it must have struck him that in the few weeks he was away his world had been turned upside down in his absence. It was not helped by the fact that he and many other critical commanders were away at the same time. He and the Commander-in-Chief of the 10th Army had been sent to collect trifling medals and be indoctrinated, another had been taken ill, and his appointed deputy had been 'foolish enough' to send the Chief of Staff on leave, a man with considerable experience replaced by a man who, by youth and inexperience, was not up to the task. Again, von Senger is polite and pleasant enough not to mention names. 'The absence of Vietinghoff, Westphal, Senger, Baade and others impaired German dexterity,' and it was senior command in Berlin which had not helped.[94]

Von Senger realised that as far the OKW (and therefore Hitler) were concerned Italy was becoming of less importance. It was, von Senger correctly believed, because of the fear that at any moment the Western Allies would land somewhere else in Europe. Von Senger also thought that the Allied inactivity in Italy was because they were building up their forces for just such a major landing somewhere in France. It was soon discovered the enemy was trying to penetrate north near Itri, and on arrival von Senger found the enemy determined in their pursuit and he had to run for cover when fired on by machine-guns.

Kesselring held a conference with the 10th Army near Sora, and when von Senger arrived he had to explain that in places his lines had not only been penetrated but some major elements of his forces were in danger of being cut off. He suggested either some form of counterattack was necessary, or to start thinking of a withdrawal (retreat). However, the main thrust of the conference was the C-Line's positioning, and how far south of the Nettuno landing it should be placed. Von Senger thought this was not making sense as it was based on the fact that the Cassino line was still holding. Von Senger in trying to read the enemy's mind thought that they would no longer bother with Cassino but simply try and outflank the area. Von Senger was critical of some changes, not least the altered chain of command, noting that his XIV Panzer Corps had been in control of operations since October 1943, and in Cassino had not only held well but developed good relationships with the other commands, but now the command areas were being split up. He believed General von Vietinghoff would have agreed with him, but as a consequence of the conference had no choice but to accept the directives. He had arranged to have holding points constructed on the Senger Line by the Todt organisation, and von Senger believed it would make an excellent rallying point if the enemy broke through, but now the forces would be lacking. There was, according to Von Senger, a lack of cohesion. Von Senger had established the 15 Panzer Grenadier Division as an essential reserve body, but it was now split into battalions in anticipation of an attack. He blamed Hitler for his continuous interference, working hundreds of miles away by looking at figures and maps, and not seeing the situation first hand. As far as von Senger was concerned the 15 Panzers had been wrongly deployed. In the safety of his headquarters Hitler could work on theory without understanding the reality of the situation. Von Senger was not the first or last German general to hold these views, but few dared utter them at the time. When the attack came von Senger believed his line would have withheld, but the redeployments and instructions meant the Germans were obliged to fight in front of their own defence system, leaving it to von Senger to try and stop the annihilation of the corps, while at the same time trying to maintain troops fighting in the Liri valley. He wrote that it was not so difficult fighting the British corps, but the French were thrusting forward with greater vigour. Von Senger thought he should advise the 10th Army to move the mobile forces as quickly as possible and form a flank at Valmontone (a municipality within the Metropolitan City of Rome in the region of Lazio, some 28 miles south-east of Rome). Von Senger believed if the enemy secured this area German forces south would be trapped. He saw Valmontone as a pivotal point for the German forces to ensure an escape route. He admitted in his memoirs he was not entirely *au fait* with all that was happening with the 10th Army, and it had only been a thought as to whether to make this point at all. When writing these memoirs, he was well aware of Field Marshal Alexander's awareness of the importance of the Valmontone position for entrapping the German army to the south, so for some cynics it may raise the question whether this viewpoint was garnered postwar or at the time. There is no way of ascertaining this cynical view except by understanding the nature of the man von Senger, which will be left for the final chapter of this study.

At this point in his memoirs von Senger paused to reflect, not least about the area in which this part of the war was being fought. He even takes his reader back to the year 1504 conflict with the French contesting the Spanish over the claims for south Italy, fighting in the same area for access to Rome and finding the same difficulties with the tough terrain, and their various failures at breaking through. He noted the French also failed when the Spanish crossed what was dubbed the Gustav Line 440 years later. He decided in his memoirs that the German attempt would be the last such effort, because in the new world the super-powers of the USSR and USA 'had started their encroachment on Central Europe…and gone are the days of independent policy by a Richelieu or a Bismark… the nations of Europe are compelled to close ranks'.[95] This thoughtful parenthesis he added sometime in the late 1950s, and it is curious regarding his political views, but more interesting regarding his historical skill in noting the way military history can be all too repetitive. He could well have advanced in his reflective asides by noting humankind's failure to learn from the past is, as many famous writers have noted, a consequence we repeat the same mistakes.

He quickly moved from this line of thought to the question of pursuing a defeated opponent, referring to the German 10th Army fleeing from Cassino and the 14th Army from Anzio. Before exploring his various viewpoints, it feels right to take an overview of the consequences of the Allied breakout from Nettuno and then return to von Senger's viewpoints.

As von Senger made clear, Kesselring's defence scheme had held months longer than the Allies had anticipated, but was now crumbling.* The German defence was being attacked at every point, and on 22 May the French made some sudden advances at Pico which some claim made 'Kesselring cry with rage'.[96] Kesselring asked for the 29th Panzer Grenadiers to be placed at the disposal of the Tenth Army, but General Mackensen was unhappy about this because he was facing a serious breakout attempt at Anzio. Kesselring became critical of Mackensen who, when he offered Kesselring his resignation for the third time at the end of May, Kesselring accepted it and replaced him with Joachim Lemelsen: 'smiling Albert remained a tough no-nonsense German General'.[97] He used Mackensen again, but it sent a warning to subordinates about reacting to orders without question. This contrasts with the American General Mark Clark and his attitude to his superior Alexander, when later, Clark deliberately disobeyed orders with incalculable consequences over his infatuation with conquering Rome, he was never reproached by Alexander.

Ultra had picked up Kesselring's message to Hitler asking permission for both armies to retreat, and for Rome to be evacuated without a fight. To avoid Rome breaking out into civil discord and uprisings, as in

* Operation *Diadem*.

Naples, Kesselring ordered that Lieutenant-General Mälzer attend a gala performance of Gigli to give the impression all was as usual. It almost beggars belief that Kesselring found time to deal with this sort of detail.[98] In breaking out from Anzio General Clark had been firmly instructed to entrap the German 10th Army by encirclement, making directly for Valmontone to block the German supply route.* Instead, in one of the worse Allied blunders, he turned into Rome to be met by Mackensen in the Alban Hills acting as a delaying line before the Caesar Defences. Clark was determined to occupy Rome at all costs and take it before the British arrived to share any glory. In his postwar memoirs Clark admitted that he intended to be the first to take Rome from the south in fifteen centuries, 'but we intended to see that the people back home knew that it was the 5th Army'.[99]

Clark's failure to close the Valmontone Gap, which could have entrapped the whole southern wing of the 10th Army, and forced some elements of the 14th Army to retreat, went against Alexander's orders in Operation *Buffalo*, and, by so doing 'he deliberately committed what must be ranked as one of the most misguided blunders made by an Allied commander during the Second World War'.[100] Clark was obsessed with ensuring the Americans arrived in Rome and was an embittered Anglophobe and his 'growing disdain for his British colleagues in Italy began to affect his judgement'.[101] Clark's planning was considered poor at Salerno, the Rapido crossing was a disaster, but in occupying Rome he made a gross error of judgement.[102] Truscott never changed his mind that Clark had made the greatest error for the sake of personal vanity. Had the Valmontone Gap been closed, and the Germans encircled, then Rome would have fallen probably more quickly than the circuitous route taken by Clark. Kesselring could see what 'Clark obsessed with his private goals could not see, that it was the combination of the Allied thrusts ... that posed the threat'.[103]

Clark arrived in Rome as the all-conquering saviour, but the failure to capture an entire German army was a serious error of judgement. Alexander was too gentlemanly, and there were no personal consequences; Kesselring had sacked Mackensen for being tardy, 'Adolf Hitler would have had him [Clark] shot'.[104] This major Allied blunder allowed Kesselring

* A major point in Operation *Diadem*.

to continue the defence for which he was becoming famous; it may well have been a very different history had Clark followed orders.

In the battle leading up to Rome the Allies lost 42,000 men and the Germans 25,000. It is apparent Kesselring was not faced with highly competent commanders on the Allied side. 'No important victory was achievable, certainly not by field commanders of such meagre abilities as Alexander and Clark'.[105] It has been believed by many that Clark 'was unfit to be an army commander', and there is little doubt by taking Rome and not entrapping the Germans forces, he gave Kesselring the means of prolonging the war in Italy to the bitter end.[106]

Alexander wrote that 'every time we attacked Kesselring in Italy we took him completely by surprise; but he showed very great skill in extricating himself from the desperate situation into which his faulty intelligence had led him'.[107] In addition to the problem of outwitting Kesselring, Alexander admitted that 'I think we may well have underestimated the remarkable resilience and toughness of the Germans'.[108] Again as early as 22 March he had written to Brooke that 'unfortunately we are fighting the best soldiers in the world – what men!'[109]

Von Senger was often critical of the Allied tactics, but he rarely mentioned the various Allied commanders. There seems little doubt from the historical postwar analysis that the German reputation for having a professional army with well-trained commanders was one of the reasons for their outstanding defences in Italy, even as the Allies drove them north. At times they were assisted by the less professional approach of the Allied commanders but still faced the overwhelming resources of the enemy. It was a twist of fate that the day Clark took Rome was the same day that the Allies arrived on D-Day Normandy. Italy remained a backwater conflict in the public eye, the fighting men were sometimes called the 'D-Day dodgers', but the fighting was tough and at times bitter, and the consequences important.

Von Senger having turned his mind to reflecting on the pursuit of the two defeated German armies, suggests it provided insights into modern war, which in a sense does not touch us in the twenty-first century as he was writing this over 70 years ago, and military technology has advanced beyond belief, but it does provide some historical perspectives worth pursuing. He noted the clash between Alexander and Clark, seeing the latter as propelled by political motives which was probably correct, but was polite not to mention Clark's egotism raised by many historians since. He believed the dual pursuit could have the intention of forcing the German enemy into a position when he is forced to capitulate without a major battle. He described how once the Gustav Line was broken the 10th Army was in the Liri valley with the French determined to make their way to Valmonte. Von Senger had wanted to head in the same direction but was ordered otherwise, and instructed to head towards Subiaco where the foothills were still open. Their main concern was avoiding the French for fear they would be forced back into the mountains, and the main effort was to avoid complete dissolution. His Italian friends the Campanaris had sought shelter in some remote monastery as the pressure intensified. Even von Senger's headquarters was emptying and having a cup of tea with General Baade and a shot-down British pilot was the last thing he did before departing.

His corps made good progress, but travelling in daylight hours was dangerous, because of the enemy's air superiority, who had also managed to destroy some bridges on the route. Von Senger wondered how far Alexander had considered separating the 14th and 10th Armies by wheeling in which may have blocked the 10th Army's escape. Even more dangerous, von Senger speculated, was if the Allied forces in the south had tried to penetrate the rear of the 10th Army. Had the Allies being able to separate the two fleeing German armies von Senger thought that this would have been catastrophic. The 14th Army managed to secure the river Tiber crossings and by rearguard action delayed the pursuit of the American 5th Army. Von Senger described all this as being 'caught up in the bustle of a war of movement'.[110] They struggled in their northward escape and eventually caught up with the 14th Army. By 10 June his most northerly division had reached Orvieto, by which time von Senger had seven divisions under his control, all having to be conducted by radio direction, but which naturally meant a good deal of improvisation by all the commanders, as individual circumstances varied all the time. They often had to move without cover and were prone to aerial attacks.

The enemy had failed to drive a wedge between the two retreating armies which may have possibly happened had General Clark followed Alexander's orders and headed for Valmontone and not Rome City. Von

Senger took some pleasure in quoting a report from the War Department in Washington written at the time which stated: 'Field Marshal Kesselring's 10th and 14th Armies, whose destruction was the goal of the struggle in Italy, were not completely destroyed, but found themselves in a headlong retreat after suffering severe losses'.[111] Von Senger noted that the Allied pursuit was not typical of a modern war, and they robbed themselves of their initial advantages.

In terms of retrospection von Senger considered the possibilities which the Allies had wasted, the first being his belief that the Allies had not realised the opportunity they had missed. He may not have known at the time the tensions between the various British and American commanders, notably the overall commander Field Marshal Alexander who had certainly hoped to isolate the 10th Army fleeing from Cassino and the Gustav Line, and the Anglophobic General Mark Clark who ignoring orders took Rome either for self-glory reasons or some political motivation. Von Senger also felt that the Allies could have used seaborne landings, but after the near disaster at Salerno and being pinned down on the beaches of Anzio this was not such an attractive policy, especially as, unknown to von Senger, all the necessary resources were being prepared for D-Day Normandy. He also added taking Sardinia would have provided them with a huge aircraft carrier.

There were changes for von Senger which he did not welcome. His XIV Panzer Corps had been deployed in the rear of the 10th Army and was therefore within the zone of the 14th Army where he was ordered to report. He had found working with the 10th Army comfortable and found this new move disturbing. He found himself with Luftwaffe units taken in by the army, with little experience of ground fighting, and also the Turkmens Division. He found them better than he had anticipated but made the telling comment that like 'many primitive peoples' although good fighters in close combat, they found it difficult to cope with artillery and aircraft, and they lacked 'the spiritual motivation' that makes people want to fight. This latter statement has to be read or understood in the light not of religious spirituality, but of fighting another nation's war.

When he reported to the 14th Army command post to General Lemelsen (General von Mackenson having been replaced for disagreeing with Kesselring) Kesselring was there and they had a three-hour conference. Von Senger took the opportunity to raise his problems of having inadequate forces at his disposal for the defence, the very place where the best troops were required. He knew that all generals like himself were constantly making such claims, but he believed that since he was the rear defence it was essential to have the best troops available. He also felt it was necessary to pull back to the Gothic Line. This was Kesselring's last major defence line set among the summits of the northern part of the Apennine Mountains. Hitler was always concerned that the Allies would outflank it with seaborne landings, so he later ordered the grand name of Gothic be changed to the Green Line which happened in June 1944. Forced labour had been used to make outposts, bunkers, and observation points. As a matter of interest, under Operation *Olive* it was breached but withdrawals were easily made, and it stayed usable until April 1945.

Von Senger believed the 10th Army was not pulled back more quickly because it was still capable of defence and slowing the Allied pursuit. Von Senger was unhappy with the decisions and course of the war, writing that these days provided some of the 'blackest moments' of his life. His staff and corps headquarters were in a wooded area in St Fiora, but quickly moved to Montalcino, which was a small hill town in the province of Siena, Tuscany. He found personal quarters with what he described as a 'landed family of lesser nobility', whose house and their physical appearance looked Germanic. His Chief of Staff had a serious car accident (which was common when travelling difficult and dangerous roads by night, and this happened to Kesselring as well), started to recover, but suddenly died from thrombosis. He had been a man Senger had liked because of his cheerful nature, and now he felt that his beloved staff of Cassino days had all gone. It was in this area von Senger heard the sad news that his son had been wounded for the eighth time, on this occasion in the forearm which had developed gangrene and his right arm had to be amputated.

In addition to all the problems he faced was the emergence of partisan warfare mainly in the rear, namely his sector, an issue of which he had hitherto been unaware. The guerrillas were constantly carrying out raids, some by blocking roads and cutting communication links. The main enemy advance had slowed because of the arrival of Panzer and a Panzer Grenadier division. This had all been helped because of the demands of the D-Day landings in Normandy, because there were fewer aircraft attacks in Italy as they were needed over France. He was not aware until after the war that the German defence had been helped by Allied divisions being withdrawn for the same reason. He realised that Italy had become a subsidiary war, the dubbed 'backwater war'. Nevertheless, despite the reduction of enemy forces the Germans were still being driven further back. From his viewpoint up a hill, he could see dozens of enemy tanks preparing to attack, and now he lacked the communication lines he had at Cassino for preparing a defence. He found himself emotionally torn between the drama of defeat and the beauty of the Tuscany landscape. His friend General Baade, as was his custom, had placed his headquarters immediately behind the front line. In the north of the Cecina, it was open countryside which provided the opportunity to resist the oncoming enemy tanks, which at least blocked an immediate breakthrough. The German Tiger tanks could only use roads, but they were useful for the retreating Germans. However, once damaged they had to be abandoned because they did not have the necessary equipment for repairs. The guerillas were quick to blow up bridges and fell trees at critical junctions. It struck von Senger that tanks were being wasted and he complained but was not heeded, because they were being sent by people who had no idea of the necessary conditions for tanks to be successful. Even in the open country of Cecina they could not hold the enemy back, just simply stall him. The best the tank could offer, von Senger noted, was to be a mobile support for infantry. As they moved north towards the river Arno, the best tactics they could offer were delaying tactics giving time for a further retreat. The Arno was the most important river in Tuscany after the Tiber. It was a difficult time for the fleeing German armies with insufficient forces for their front lines, with the issues ever present with motor vehicles of all types. They were fighting their southern lines with what von Senger called mere battle-worthy patrols, making for a weak rearguard. They also needed mobile reserves to back up areas which had come under serious pressure, and essential radio communications when to break off and catch up with the major forces. The main force may have successfully withdrawn some 30 kilometres, but for mutual safety the rearguard guard elements had to break off to keep up. Once the rearguard was near the main forces, they could then take up their position so the army could move further on;

it was all a matter of harmonising the various movements and timing. Naturally the fighting became fiercer as they approached the formidable barrier of the river Arno. Von Senger knew that before the Arno was reached the fighting had to be decisive, because it was anticipated the Arno would become a significant battle line. He also recognised there had to be time to make sure the Arno line could be as well-established as possible given the limited time parameters.

Von Senger described the dangers of the constant enemy attacks with the main defence carried out by the 26 and 90 Panzer, and when he needed to visit Baade's headquarters, he had to pass through the constant barrage of shells trying to find safe places in the woodland thickets. He placed in his memoirs a letter he wrote to Baade's army newspaper commending him personally for the quality of his fighting troops on the defence, writing, 'however great the exertions, however strong the enemy, however serious our own losses, I was always greeted by cheerful faces. This gave me renewed strength for my own task, I thank the division and all the soldiers whom I got to know during these days of battle'.[112]

When his corps eventually reached the Arno, the enemy was busy destroying bridges in their rear which Von Senger did not think raised a crisis. The river was low, and this helped them build a few ford-bridges, which were easily concealed from aerial spotter planes. The river was a natural and difficult barrier which could be defended, it was not easy for tanks, and they all hoped for a moment of peace. On 16 July his Corps headquarters moved into the vicinity of Pistoria where it stayed for a whole month. He had a swimming pool, the weather was hot, but he did not like the new quarters because they lacked any sense of homeliness. His journeys to the front now became more tours of inspection, and he even found time to visit Pisa which was technically in the front line but with no fighting. He wrote a few paragraphs in his memoirs relating to the beauty of the area and its towns, often, as was his habit, commenting on their religious sites and their history.

He soon heard that the OKW was wondering how long the Arno position could be held, which was unlike the high command who normally never thought of withdrawal until it was seriously breached, and von Senger heard, they were still preparing the Gothic Line. Von Senger found the Arno line too exposed, but he knew that Kesselring always wanted to spare Italian towns and Florence was dangerously close, and they did not have the resources to feed the population. Von Senger was in full agreement thinking it would be wrong to destroy such ancient heritages which would be inevitable when desperation was reached, as had already been seen in the destruction of the Monte Cassino Abbey. He was also concerned about the priceless pieces of art stored in various places in the locality. Even in the smaller towns and villages there were priceless frescos. He named them and the artist exhibiting his wide education. Even in his own headquarters they found works of art they did their best to make safe. It was at this juncture he wrote of some people's cynicism provoked by Göring's 'special commandos' on the lookout for treasures he liked to keep in his own collection.

However, von Senger noted that the retreat area was dangerous because it was so open providing no cover from air attack. He was also aware that there were now different groups of partisans, some controlled by the British, others by the dreaded communists. He mentioned that Red Cross lorries could be stopped by one group of partisans, checked, and allowed to move on, first warning them there were Red Partisans further along the road. This provoked considerable anger among the German troops who had been taught that apart from all the other dangers partisans were illegal, and it was known that some German troops had carried out dreadful reprisals. Von Senger knew later that in places the treatment of partisans was barbaric, and after the war the issues would be raised in many trials based on war criminality. It was inevitable that the partisans avoided the reprisals which tended to fall entirely upon innocent citizens. These actions caused even more antagonism towards the Germans who in places quickly became hated. Von Senger did his best to stop this, not just the killing, but forcing people to be informers, and throwing families out of their homes. He admitted it was not easy to control, especially because many of his men had not been under his command for long, and some were not under his jurisdiction nor his discipline. The partisan war in Italy, as with that in Eastern Europe and the resistance in France was becoming tougher and more bitter by the day, and it would create a sense of hatred on all sides of the divides. Von Senger was acutely aware that Italy remained politically unstable and divided. There were Italians fighting Italians, others fighting the Germans and some the Allies. The

Blackshirt Brigades were disliked and after the war there would be many recriminations both in the courts and at the personal level. Reprisals, hostages, divided communities, families, and blood feuds were becoming all too characteristic in Italian life. Von Senger noted the war was no longer merely military, but a 'politico-military one' and felt this implied an impending termination. He also knew that from the German perspective the war was lost, the Russians pushing west, the Allies fighting in France, and in Italy he had spent months in defence and being pursued by the enemy. Because of the partisans he moved his headquarters because there had been assassinations of senior German officers, and nowhere felt safe. At one point the front was reasonably quiet but they 'were infested' with partisans. He found some pleasure watching the vineyards being harvested and some signs of Autumn.

He was at his temporary headquarters in Pistoria when the 20 July Plot by Count von Stauffenberg failed. He wrote in his memoirs he had known about the plot and had discussed it with some intimate friends, always warning that it could not work. It was a knowledge which was dangerous to affirm at the time, but a safety valve after the war. Kesselring claimed ignorance, but mentions that Dr Karl Gördeler had tried to 'approach me in 1942, but unsuccessfully, as I could not then be reached'.[113] Dollmann confirmed this, referring to Gördeler as 'a ringleader'.[114] When it was safe after the war, Kesselring conceded to his son that he was aware 'that something was afoot'.[115] Westphal and von Senger knew about the plot, and von Senger had informed Kesselring's son that he owed his life to Kesselring's intervention at that difficult time.[116] It also appears Kesselring saved another senior officer, two in all, it may have been Westphal or even von Vietinghoff.[117]

Von Senger understood that the conspiracy had to be kept secret amongst the few who were active, and his anxiety now focused on what would happen to the conspirators. He knew they would have to pay with their lives, and he would later be shocked when he heard of the thousands who suffered as a result of passing through the Peoples Court of Judge Freisler. Von Senger made some comments on a politically divided Italy, but Germany, he observed, had not been stable for years. There had always been those who opposed Hitler for whom Dachau was opened as soon as Nazism came to power, others who had supported his promises of a better future but who had changed their minds on seeing the barbarities of the regime, and many more who also had doubts when the war started to turn in 1943. Nazism was so evil many were silent from sheer fear, and there was always that element who supported Hitler to the bitter end, the fanatics. Von Senger wrote in his memoirs that he was personally acquainted with Stauffenberg and some of his family and his friends, who although not involved in the plot suffered the consequences of just knowing the plotters. If what von Senger stated in his memoirs about his own views is trustworthy, then his views would have been known by some senior Nazis. His attending the indoctrination course in the midst of a military crisis in Italy may well have indicated he had been put on the possible suspects' lists. His saving option was that for months he had been up to his eyeballs close to the frontline, and totally preoccupied in defence, often having to duck for cover himself. He knew that Stauffenberg had organised the last effort, but that other men he admired like Generals Beck and Oster and many others had been unhappy about the Nazi regime since its inception. Von Senger looked to the fact that many of the conspirators came from the general staff, and he decided that they would rather go under than defile themselves on moral grounds, not mentioning that some were more concerned about a looming defeat because of Hitler's ridiculous military directions.

After the war he was angry with those historians who for one reason or another 'scoffed' at the effort as being useless or too late and unrealistic. Understandably, and correctly from this writer's viewpoint, the plot demonstrated that not all Germans were pro-Nazi, and their failed efforts brought some comfort to postwar Germany. He wondered at the time or postwar whether this should mean capitulation, and probably unknown to him one of the leading and highly respected civilian leaders of the Kreisau Circle, which was headed by the jurist Helmuth James von Moltke, tended to have thought the same way even before the plot failed, knowing that with 'unconditional surrender' in the air, it was too late for negotiations.

In his memoirs he tried to justify what would appear his own passive attitude to the resistance movement. He admitted that 'outwardly' he appeared to take no notice of the news of the plot, and crushed the rumour that when the news arrived, he was playing the card game Bridge and simply said 'I Pass', denying this and stating that he had never played Bridge in his life. He pointed out that his NSFO (National Socialist leadership officer) had criticised him for not raising his arm in the correct way for the Hitler salute. He was concerned about the reaction of the troops and their morale and made no mention or took any attitude before them. He noted that unlike the Great War there was no crumbling of morale, but the military side was in disarray. He was a realist and admitted that 'it would have been suicidal to champion the conspirators'.[118] In his memoirs he found it sad that the reaction of the public was minimal, but as he feared taking sides could be suicidal for a general, it was the same for the public who knew of the dangers of the Gestapo using informants and denouncers to weed out and execute opposition. He attacked the lack of political astuteness of the Germans, but there were two elements he overlooked. First, when Hitler rose to power Germany was in a terrible economic state and regarded as a pariah nation, and Hitler's promises of a better future of work, better pay, better living conditions paved the way and never mentioned war and genocide. Secondly, once in power the Gestapo and Himmler's SS turned the German people into a state of total subjugation and repression, as von Senger must have known when he stated it was best to keep quiet.

Von Senger did notice some changes amongst his soldiers, as if by knowing that not every officer had been pro-Hitler, it appeared to raise questions in their minds as to their and the country's long-term future. At this stage in his memoirs, he pauses again as if to take stock of his own world views. He noted the impossibility of Russia not paying attention to the will of the people and where crimes had taken place to secure the Soviet leadership. He believed the Germans had fallen even lower by liquidating people based on race and religion. It was curious at this stage he did not mention the Russian massacre at Katyń, which when he was writing was still denied by the Soviets.

Once his mind reverted to where he was in Italy, he admitted from mid-September to October was depressing. His own corps was on the right wing of the 14th Army on what he described as the dead sector of the front. It struck him that the enemy was short of divisions which was probably true because of the war in France, and that the British were launching coastal raids along the Adriatic coastline, as it offered flat plains making landing that much easier. Generally, they did not work and von Senger was pleased to note that he had previously observed the problem for armoured tanks in such terrain. The US 5th Army was attacking again from Florence trying to break through towards Bologna, which was of more concern than the British coastal raids. From his particular geographical position von Senger was not seeing much fighting, as it was the left wing of the 14th Army which was bearing the brunt. A moment of self-conceit creeps into his memoirs at this stage as he believed with his Cassino experience, he could do a better job than the more recently appointed senior commanders. He was evidently at this stage ruminating on the point of battling away in a lost cause, writing that 'it is quite possible to condemn a war for its futility or its hopeless strategic concepts, and yet to be impelled towards the decisive battleground through the inescapable force of destiny'.[119] Von Senger was always in danger, but not as much as the frontline soldier, many of whom, on all sides must have often wondered why they were fighting under the circumstances. He ensured his own safety when travelling by doing so in a small Volkswagen and displaying no signs of rank, having seen a colleague do otherwise, and being killed by the partisans. Despite his views on the political situation, he gave the impression of being bored in his current situation, as all he could do was listen to the news about the fighting from elsewhere. Many of his experienced soldiers would have been pleased with the situation. Almost like an excited schoolboy he heard on 15 October that it was about change and he 'could join the fray', this was because the Commander-in-Chief of the 14th Army had been ill for five days and von Senger was to take his place. Again, with a sense of conceit, he felt during this time he managed to halt the US 5th Army on its advance towards Bologna. There may well have been some truth in this as Kesselring sent a letter of congratulations to him.

At the end of October, he moved his headquarters to Vedrana where he hoped he would be at the centre of events. He took over the area previously occupied by the LI Mountain Corps, but on 20 November the British 8th Army started its offensive and his corps was weakened because of the constant shifting of units to fill the gaps. It is clear from von Senger's account that the quiet period was now over, as in early January the enemy had pushed as far as Lake Comacchio (Comacchio is better known as a lagoon and is a vast area of brackish water) and units were swapped and changed at a moment's notice. Senger's own corps was weakened by the hasty rearrangements which he knew he had to accept under the circumstances, but in his opinion still remained capable. Von Senger even arranged quick courses for new commanding officers in defence, based on his experience at Cassino. He was also concerned about the defensive line as it failed to conform to his rules about mountain warfare. He needed to make changes which he admitted had to be confirmed by the OKW or kept secret from them. The terrain was complex with the rivers Reno and Setta with broad valleys running south to Bologna, with mountain summits which would spell disaster if the enemy gained them. Von Senger sent out raiding parties at night to bring in prisoners, evidently for the sake of intelligence. As the early months of 1945 passed von Senger became more critical of the nature of their defence and saw the chances of a good defence becoming less and less. Later von Senger was able to read Alexander's account which expressed the belief that the Germans had a strong defence line and would be too costly to attack.

In Bologna

The operation of taking Bologna was difficult from the operational perspective, but feeding a major population was almost out of the question. It appeared that both sides had serious issues. The towns had produced considerable partisan activity, and von Senger admitted some of the reprisals had been excessive, even water and electric supplies had been stopped. Bologna was an important hub for roads and railways, as well as being an industrial centre, and had been a target for extensive Allied bombing raids which destroyed much of the ancient area of the city. By the end of the war, it was estimated that a massive 44 per cent of buildings had been destroyed or seriously damaged. It was also recognised as a key centre for partisans. Von Senger thought correctly that the Allies considered it too costly to occupy.

Von Senger, like many other commanders regarded the partisans as gangsters, a form of underworld trying to rule the city. According to von Senger, and probably with a degree of truth some civilians were murdered by partisans, either because they were seen as informants, were fascist, friendly with the Germans, and sometimes for personal reasons. Von Senger noted they would pin a label reading SPIA on their victims meaning the corpse had been a German spy. Von Senger's animosity increased with his belief that most of the partisans were communist which is impossible to ascertain. He had no sympathy for them even though they were fighting the occupier. They were sometimes helped by German deserters, not least for acquiring weapons and information. It is curious that a few pages earlier von Senger had written about the high morale of the German troops and later, when in Bologna referred to the problems of German deserters. When he wrote about the sense of questioning faces after the 20 July Plot, he should have wondered whether some of these deserting soldiers were beginning to wonder whether the Nazi regime was worth dying for. There are hundreds of reasons for desertion, but the moral stance may well have applied to some. Being in control of such a large city with its mixed political attitudes in the middle of a war was no easy task, so rather than leave it to some subordinate, von Senger set himself up as the main commandant. He put one of his senior officers in charge who had to report to von Senger twice a week. It was in this office that von Senger would meet the city's administration officers. They were a mixed group; the Prefect was young and von Senger thought he might still believe in a German victory. In contrast, Mayor Agnoli had no political interests, his main concern was the welfare of the city. Another was a Mussolini man, but on the whole it appeared that von Senger liked them as a group to work alongside.

Von Senger found the Guardia Republicana Nazionale, one of the new Republican-Fascist organisations all too keen to join the fighting, and when von Senger organised this, he was told they fought well. On the other hand, von Senger found the *Camicie Nere* (the Blackshirts) like many others difficult. They were dedicated fascists who recruited all the extremists and disliked by most people. They represented for them, the one and only ruler, Mussolini. They would think nothing of murdering political opponents and had no time for von Senger and his administration, as they felt their real colleagues were Himmler's SS and SD. It was ironic that one of the main supporters behind the Blackshirts was a professor of the university's medical faculty, who had no time for the city administrators nor von Senger.

None of this discordant political backdrop was helped when in late November four prominent civilians had been murdered because it was known they were anti-fascist. The population tended to blame these murders on the professor, but there was no proof because he was astute enough to keep his influence well in the background. It was awkward for von Senger because as much as he despised the Blackshirts, they were helping the Germans in their fight against the partisans. The professor also had the support of the German Ambassador (Rahn) to Mussolini, and von Senger knew that if he arrested the man, it would be seen as a political misdemeanour. Von Senger found that Rahn was sympathetic to the issues with which he was dealing, but lurking in the background was Ribbentrop who preferred the tougher stance taken by von Senger's predecessors. Von Senger saw a strange dichotomy in this advice, because normally the military commander had to be prepared to be ruthless, and the diplomatic service should have been trying to maintain good relationships, but Ribbentrop had reversed the roles. Ribbentrop was generally despised by most people. In his diary, the Italian foreign minister Ciano spent pages disparaging him, and Hassell in his diary described him as giving 'insane leadership' and as becoming totally 'rabid'.[120] He was initially admired by Hitler who sometimes referred to him as the 'second Bismarck'. This remark was noted by many on several occasions when Hitler had been asked about his foreign minister, but this response related not to Ribbentrop's brilliance but his subservience to Hitler who gave all the necessary directions.

Despite the warnings von Senger decided to act over the dangerous professor, telling him that he and his associates were banned from Bologna, on the excuse that the city was on the frontline and their departure was necessary to maintain a sense of order. This did bring some stability, according to von Senger, and many welcomed this confrontation with the Blackshirts who had brought such concern to the citizens. He found consequently he had problems with Himmler's SD as they took this as a personal insult, having seen the professor as being under their wings. Von Senger found himself in the same position as many Wehrmacht commanders who while fighting in the frontline, found that they had the SD acting as policemen, when an operational zone should have been entirely under the control of the fighting army. Later von Senger discovered that Himmler had demanded his dismissal, and he had only escaped this by the interference of General Friedrich Wolff, the senior SS commander in Italy and backed by Kesselring. It would be this General Wolff who later arranged the surrender of German troops in Italy. In the meantime, von Senger tried to lessen the authority of the SS in the war zones, and in his own autobiography it appears that Kesselring held the same views. Even when offences occurred against German troops von Senger attempted to have the case held in ordinary civilian courts. Kesselring had tried to ensure the safety of Italian towns and cities where possible, and he had wanted Bologna nominated as an 'Open City'. On these grounds von Senger at one time ordered that German troops should stay out of the city centre, but also with the clever intention or excuse of making it easier to deal with the partisans. The bombing of the town centre ceased and von Senger realised the inhabitants thought the two sides had reached an agreement which was not the case. Von Senger believed both the Vatican and Badoglio government had used their influence. This also meant that von Senger had to create some rearward defence lines. There was confusion between what the civilian population thought and the reality of the day, and von Senger asked Kesselring to either cancel the rearward defence system or inform the mayor there was no international agreement. As it transpired there was no need because the enemy's offensive plans did not include taking Bologna. Because civilians believed Bologna to be neutral there was an understandable influx of refugees. The farmers had brought their stock in and the issue of feeding the population was made easier by this action, and the only shortage was salt over which von Senger ordered military supplies to help. Von Senger also stopped the installation of brothels for troops, not least because they never benefitted front line troops and created venereal disease problems. Von Senger had become the understood Commandant of Bologna and his diplomatic skills had, according to many pieces of evidence, made him acceptable to many Italians, even though most were looking forward to seeing the back of the Germans.

Von Senger made a friend of a former professor at Bologna university who had lost a son and was bitterly anti-fascist, and following a directive that the Germans should cooperate with the Church as they cared for the starving, he paid a formal visit to the Archbishop, a Cardinal Count

Naselli Rocca. Von Senger soon found the senior cleric had an antipathy to the Germans, which should not have been too surprising. It remained formal as von Senger discovered that his mastery of the Italian language and his Catholic faith did not help matters. He found it more helpful when meeting a Father Casati, the Prior of the Dominican Convention who appeared more sympathetic. Von Senger saw in him a man of some intellect and education, finding him more cooperative.

By this stage it appeared to von Senger that they had created a stable front, but everyone knew that the Germans had lost, and their situation was rapidly deteriorating. It was quiet enough for von Senger to wander around bookshops and ride alone into the beautiful countryside. His staff and even Italian friends warned him of the dangers, but he ignored them, writing that 'the disgruntled partisans let it be known that they would do me no harm'.[121] It is impossible to ascertain whether this was true or von Senger's hopeful imagination, but there may be some truth in his judgement. One historian pointed out with some justification that his attempt to save the Abbey and his care for churches had earned him the respect of the Italians and even the partisans 'who never attacked him during his many trips through the Italian countryside'.[122]

It was a possibility that the partisans had seen progress in the city with von Senger at the helm, but that remains sheer speculation. He organised with some difficulty for the Bologna Opera to reopen, and as a compensation for closing the brothels arranged for German soldiers to attend the performances. Quite how this alternative offer of attending opera performances for brothel visits went down with the average soldier is not difficult to imagine. He opened an officers' club, a cinema, held concerts and some military education courses. For reasons he did not explain he had to move his headquarters in early January to a house (where the previous occupant had been murdered by the partisans) which he found less pleasant, mainly because the furnishings were in his opinion of bad taste. He brightened the place up by arranging with the Italian authorities to borrow seven pictures of the seven sacraments. There could have been little doubt among his staff about his deep religious feelings.

He was surprised by the climate in that latitude, he had described how he often returned from the frontlines frozen, trudging his way through snow back to his small cold Volkswagen. He was grateful to return to his warm rooms. His soldiers may have been freezing, but reading von Senger's memoirs it gives the appearance that he felt as if he were on holiday. He noted that when the thaw set in, they could even drink their coffee in the orchard attached to the property, and he even sent for his horses. This description of his daily life indicates he was now in a backwater war because the war in Europe on both the Eastern and Western fronts was raging with Germany's borders in danger. He even arranged to have a horse jumping course laid out. He knew the enemy was closing in but rejoiced he had time to write to his children and could still talk to them by telephone.

However, he was aware that his troops were on edge, and he was worried about their spiritual and mental well-being. The soldiers, at least most of them, knew the war was lost whether they could hold the defence south of the Alps or not. He did not mention that many of them would have families in Germany who were not only facing relentless bombing, but invading foreign armies which must have played incessantly on their minds. This alone may have accounted for some of the desertions. He carefully selected his own NSFO officer (Nazi leadership officer like the Russian Commissar) a man who had little to do with the Party, with whom he felt free to discuss all the difficulties of the time. This was preferable he noted from having to deal with the usual fanatical Nazis often selected for this post. After the 20 July Plot the higher authorities were almost paranoid about a repetition and were suspicious of all officers, especially new appointments. Von Senger never had this appointment confirmed, which was a demand of the Party regulations, and von Senger refused to have him replaced. The Party sent an inspector to investigate the situation, but higher command accepted the appointment. It is almost unbelievable that in the closing months of the war when even the wonder weapons had proved to be sheer nonsense, that high command found time to worry about this appointment in faraway Bologna. Von Senger believed he had fooled the officials, and he kept the indoctrination of the troops in his own hands. He also ensured other NSFOs in other units had little time to work at their designated business. Von Senger decided there were two types of NSFO, first the fanatical and the informers whom everyone feared, and the second were more of the decent type, with von Senger urging his commanders to avoid the first type. The propaganda department provided maps which seemed to indicate the Germans still held more territory than the enemy, but von Senger knew these maps fooled no one, and indeed did more damage to the Party propaganda than they could have foreseen. Von Senger knew that the Nazi success had been evident between 1939 and 1942, but from 1943 it had turned into a defensive war, and by 1944 the more astute soldiers knew the war was lost. Von Senger was disturbed by the rumour that in the dying days Hitler would seek refuge in the southern Alps and it would be his soldiers who would be called to fight to the end. Few now believed the rumours of deadly weapons such as death-rays, and not all soldiers believed everything they were told, even many of the Nazi fanatics were beginning to see the future in a different light. Another aspect von Senger ruminated on was the general ignorance by even anti-fascist officers who knew about the criminality of the Nazi regime. For many of them Hitler was still the rightful leader to whom they had pledged obedience and some of them did not seek any form of capitulation. Men who held these views von Senger found the least dependable.

Chapter 5

The Last Days

Kesselring, being known as a master of defence had been reassigned for the western defence in France and Germany against the Allies, and General von Vietinghoff had taken his place as Commander-in-Chief of Army Group C and warned the OKW that the Apennine front would not be able to withstand a major enemy offensive. Von Senger remained concerned about his XIV Panzer Corps because he was certain it would have to confront a main thrust by the enemy, but senior command was uncertain about which direction the Allied armies would take, but believed Bologna would be in their plans. However, he noted that the enemy had made no efforts during Autumn, and he wondered whether the army move from Lake Comacchio would eventually lead him towards Verona. It was clear that in the Italian battle area all had gone relatively quiet, and von Senger would not have been the only German commander wondering what was going to happen next and where. He felt his troops still had a good fighting spirit, but he lacked the necessary mobility of motorised divisions.

The attack started on 14 April 1945, and came as a surprise against the right wing of his corps, but he felt it was more a diversionary tactic although the enemy gained considerable land and advances. When the enemy suddenly wheeled von Senger had reserves ready, but the pressure was too much. He was unhappy about the way the reserves had been used because some had been sent to deal with partisan problems, and no counterattack could be raised. Von Senger managed to establish a small form of operational front, but he knew it had no backbone. He noted the partisans in Bologna remained almost subdued, and rightly or wrongly decided that it was because his administration in that city had been welcomed. He moved his headquarters, but nobody could move by day because the enemy Air Force dominated the skies. Even his long-term batman Feuerstak was wounded in an air attack when using a barrow to fetch provisions; von Senger sat with him in hospital holding his hand as he had to have a leg amputated. They had been together for seven years, but this injury meant the end of a long working relationship. In his memoirs he knew that Feuerstak was leading some form of peasant's life in the Eastern zone, the GDR.

On 20 April von Senger's headquarters were attacked by enemy aircraft indicating that they knew his whereabouts, the bombs exploded close by, but he was unharmed. It amounted to a military fiasco as he felt chased from one place to another. In the area south of the river Po, as he had noted earlier, there was no cover or place to hide, and the enemy air superiority was proving devastating.

Two days later on 22 April, he had to decide whether to be taken prisoner with corps staff or cross the Po. He decided to cross the river and his staff were dissolved into different groups. There were a few ferries left, but they could not operate during the day, and many men swam across the river. He managed a ferry trip and marched some 15 miles to Legnano where he was unable to establish any contacts. Von Senger and his few men spent the night of 23 April there with the intention of crossing the river Adige (Italy's second longest river) to reach the corps base at St Stefano. The bridges had been destroyed and movement by day was proving impossible. When he arrived, he managed to assemble his corps staff from those who had made it there. During the night of the 24 April, they tried to make their way through the Adige valley but were held up by traffic blockages and obstacles. They managed during the next night and installed their battle headquarters in a remote mountain village called Ronchi. Some other units arrived, and they tried to set up a defensive front from Lake Garda to the Pasubio pass, a place known to have some 52 tunnels and faced by sheer rock faces. However, it appeared the enemy attacks were slowing down, and von Senger wondered if they had decided not to waste more lives. The roads were packed with stragglers which for von Senger was a sign of total dissolution and disbanding. Von Senger insisted it was not a loss of morale as he knew they were returning to anticipated supply bases. This seemed to be a huge assumption by von Senger, because most of these soldiers could work out for themselves that not only was the war lost but most would know that Western Allied and Soviet troops were deep in Germany.

Eventually von Senger arrived at the Blue Line which was a solid form of defence system dating back to the First World War with deep fortifications. He spent the nights of 29 and 30 April lodging in the house of a Count Frederigotti near Roverto, who was also giving space to a senior Todt official who wanted to surrender. His host belonged to the Italian Committee of Liberation which von Senger saw as his right and duty. On 1 May he moved his lodgings to Matterello (south of Trent) and found lodgings in a beautiful villa, but only two days before moving around again. What he did not know at the time was in higher quarters there were serious divisions of opinions about whether to fight on or capitulate.

The Surrender and Imprisonment

The SS General Karl Wolff under Operation *Sunrise* was working with intermediaries to make contact in Switzerland with Allen W. Dulles with a view to surrendering German troops in Italy. These meetings had started as early as March 1945, and Wolff arranged for the surrender to be signed on 29 April which became effective on 2 May, a mere week before the surrender in Germany. This whole venture of which von Senger was unaware offers some curious and relevant insights into the machinations about the efforts to finish the war in Italy, and the fraught relationship between the SS command and the Wehrmacht.

Earlier on when Kesselring had been in direct command, Wolff had approached Kesselring with the idea that the SS performed police duties within the army-controlled area. From 1934 von Senger and Kesselring had been accustomed to living within a police state, 'a category of political regime in which the police, the security services and the special forces were authorised to bypass the normal procedures of the law'.[1] As such Kesselring nearly accepted the offer, but was warned off by Westphal, who was more averse to the SS than Kesselring. As Westphal later noted, 'not even a field-marshal of the Army was permitted to punish a soldier of these forces with a single day's arrest. The Army authorities could do no more than make representations to Göring or Himmler'.[2] There was command-confusion, and by 1 May 1944 Kesselring had demanded that Keitel send a signal defining his duties; Kesselring was made the highest authority, but the partisan war was given to *Obergruppenführer* Wolff and his guerrilla operations staff. They were subordinate to Kesselring only for the sake of military appearances.

The question has often been raised as to what was happening in mainland Europe which was of greater consequence than the German Army stuck in northern Italy. The answer might be found in the growing western fear of communist incursion, which was kept silent as the Russians were then important allies. The same concern about communist motives was felt on the German side: Wolff, Dollmann and Rahn believed that with French communists in the west, Tito to the east there would be a communist block and they believed 'the only solution was to arrange an orderly surrender of German forces'.[3] It was probably this underlying concern about communism that in Switzerland SS General Wolff held secret meetings with Allen Dulles to finish the war in Italy for fear of a communist take-over.* Harold Macmillan claimed that 'the first indications that some of Kesselring's officers wished to treat for terms had reached us on 8 March' and that Wolff, together with an OKW representative, was presumably from Kesselring's staff, the latter point about the OKW was only Macmillan's speculation.[4] The British assumed that Kesselring was cognisant, and Dollmann, postwar claimed he was.[5] Wolff visited Kesselring on 23 March to persuade him to allow Vietinghoff to surrender. Kesselring was obviously aware of this operation which the Allies had code-named '*Sunrise*'.** Following a row with Wolff, Kesselring had 'backed the steps that were being taken and agreed to be associated with them' but added 'that an end only came into question for him if the Führer were no longer alive'.[6]

---

* It was suggested that Wolff was not seeking peace, but working for Himmler to create problems with Stalin's paranoia that the West was making peace. When Wolff sent an optimistic message to Dulles that Kesselring was ready for further discussion it has been suggested it 'was intended for Stalin's agents'. See Peter Padfield, *Himmler Reichs Führer-SS* (London: Cassell & Co, 2001), pp.574–6.

** The Americans appeared to trust Wolff and when later 'Nuremberg prosecutors gathered three folders of evidence relevant to Wolf's administrative involvement in war crimes, including the extermination of European Jewry', he still found protection from Dulles, see Michael Salter, *Nazi War Crimes, US Intelligence and Selective Prosecution at Nuremberg* (Oxford: Routledge-Cavendish, 2007), p.25.

Kesselring's hesitancy was obtuse; he dismissed Vietinghoff for surrendering because Hitler still lived, which given what was happening was, as Kershaw wrote, a 'graphic case' of following 'insane orders'.[7] It was unlikely to be Kesselring's fear of Hitler's wrath, but his fanatical brutality in that not only did he dismiss Vietinghoff, but 'he ordered his arrest and execution'.* The obsession with obeying Hitler was typical of the higher command, as von Hassell wrote in his 1943 diary: 'none of the Field Marshals is acting as if he knew any higher concept of duty'.[8] Originally it may have been that Kesselring was seeking an immunity deal from Dulles, as he had investigated 'Swiss citizenship', but the delays were poor judgement.[9] Kesselring undoubtedly still felt 'bound by his oath despite Hitler's death'.[10]

Von Senger, admiring the Italian landscape and its beautiful ancient buildings while fleeing for his life was totally unaware of these machinations. He eventually heard from General Lemelsen that Kesselring, deep in France, had ordered that von Vietinghoff be transferred and the command given to a General Schutz (unknown to von Senger). Later he was told that on 1 May Schulz had been arrested and Lemelsen was now taking over, who had received written instructions from Kesselring prohibiting negotiations with the enemy without a special order. The same day von Senger was ordered by Lemelsen to take over the army headquarters at Fay, where he was given a slightly confusing picture of the situation as General Schulz and his colleague General Wenzel had suddenly been freed. He finally heard that the surrender would come into force at 2 p.m. on 2 May and could not be rescinded. The commanders of the 10th and 14th armies and Luftwaffe had no choice. Von Senger felt he had not received adequate clarification, and he checked with his friend General Wenzel and was told it had all been settled in an 'honourable way'. Von Senger, who had been in the dark about these arrangements still felt unconvinced until General Lemelsen confirmed it for him over the phone. He also heard that Hitler had died in Berlin, upon which von Senger speculated that at this news fighting would stop on all fronts.

* Richard Raiber, *Anatomy of Perjury* (Delaware: Delaware Press, 2008), p.180. Vietinghoff was released in 1947 and helped in West Germany's rearmament, by writing the Himmerod Memorandum.

Von Senger sent out his orders in line with his superiors, and he heard no objections.

On the morning of 2 May he gathered his troops and officers together and explained the situation. He was concerned that some might want to fight on, so he drew their attention to the sheer hopelessness of the situation. He explained their lack of resources, the power of the enemy, and the way the situation had deteriorated since Cassino. He even reminded them of many of the senseless orders they had received to hold to positions which they knew to be a dangerous waste of time and life. He then added that the much-loved and respected commander Kesselring had given his approval, which was a tenuous statement as Kesselring was not happy at surrender while Hitler lived, but either way he had no choice by this stage. Then, typically of von Senger, he took a walk in the countryside. On his return he was told he had to lead a mission to General Mark Clark (now commander the 15th Army Group) to execute the instrument of surrender. He was accompanied by some selected staff and drove to Bolzano (capital city in the province of South Tyrol) headquarters for the details. Earlier a Lieutenant Colonel Schweinitz, following the total defeat of the Germans on the river Po had established a couple of formal concessions, one being the temporary retention of sidearms by officers, but signed under the agreement that it had to be countersigned by the commander-in-chief. Kesselring's agreement was somewhat elastic, as noted earlier, he needed confirmation that the Führer was dead. Some troops were asking if Dönitz (Hitler's nominated successor) had agreed to surrendering weapons, and von Senger realised the possibility that some might want to fight on regardless of the consequences. There was even the question of the hope that the West's distaste of Soviet communism might be utilised by the Germans, but this remained a forlorn if not wasted hope.

On 3 May, von Senger attended a meeting between General Wolff and the leader of the South Tyrol Liberation committee who wanted the transfer of the local power to the Italian government. Wolff had no choice but to object, as he pointed out that such decisions now rested with the Allies. Von Senger was aware of firing going on between German troops and the Tyrolese freedom fighters, and that Bolzano was surrounded by Tyrol liberation troops which had its earlier start in 1809. He received a message that a British colonel had called to see him, so he invited him to Balzano where they had a 'correct and pleasant' lunch together. The British colonel and a general had been sent by General Clark to collect von Senger, but they had become lost in the Tyrolese effort of fighting for their freedom. The American General Ruffner eventually arrived and von Senger played the host by offering a cup of tea. That evening at 8 p.m. accompanied by von Schweinitz who had signed the original act of surrender, they moved off to their meeting. They had to walk the last part because of the rubble, and American soldiers carried their luggage. They were transported across a stormy Lake Garda in an amphibious vehicle. On arrival they transferred to a large American car, and he was met by a General Hay. Because of von Senger's good English language skills they exchanged reminiscences about the fighting, and he discovered that their respective troops had met in battle. It had been a cold and wet journey finally resting in a well-known hotel in Verona.

On 4 May they had an English breakfast, by which von Senger probably meant a 'fry-up' and thanked the British liaison officer whom he addressed as Mr John Profumo, not using his rank but drawing attention to the politician. His German memoirs came out in 1960 and it is unlikely that he was alluding to the Profumo scandal because it was 1961 when Profumo met Christine Keeler. From there they were flown to Florence, and they were greeted with what von Senger described as 'prescribed protocol'. As he entered Clark's presence, von Senger stepped on the American General's pet spaniel which returned the greeting by biting his ankle. It was not a preliminary prediction for the meeting, as he found the meeting genial and without any ill-feeling. He was asked to report to Clark alone, and a 'pleasant officer' hinted to him the right approach. He suggested that von Senger explain that he had the authority of his senior commander to accept the surrender, but he did not mention unconditional surrender, which the Allied radio broadcasts were repeatedly warning. Clark was in his tent under the American flag and flanked by the commanders of the US 5th Army and the British 8th. His impression was that for his one-time opponents it was painful because they saw him as the representative of the Nazi regime. They would not know of von Senger's anti-Nazi attitudes, but as for himself, he wrote that it had marked the end of twelve years of spiritual servitude. He found Clark intelligent and pleasant, and at the meeting raised the issue of the liberation troops in the Tyrol causing havoc and problems. The liberation troops had only started fighting when the surrender was known, and this was difficult for the German troops who had to defend themselves. Clark agreed it was difficult for the Germans to surrender their weapons while under such a threat. The negotiations were not made easy by Allied aeroplanes spotting German troops and vehicles moving north towards Brenner which was an infringement of the surrender terms. There was also evidence that 1 Para Corps were continuing to fight which von Senger had always feared. All von Senger could add was that these actions ran counter to the intentions of his own commander-in-chief, and the partisans were stopping his commander-in-chief from acting against these problems. The radio unit sent to help von Senger stay in touch had not arrived, and later he discovered they had been rounded up and placed in a PoW camp. Nor were the Germans happy with bringing troops back to the Bologna region as they thought this might be dangerous, and this could lead to many desertions. He found Clark somewhat sympathetic to his points, explaining that this had been felt right because of the supply problems. Clark promised to defer his decisions given the points raised, and he demanded there should not be any press announcements. For the next few days negotiations were at a standstill, and von Senger was given a small house in which to rest with American rations.

In his own memoirs Clark presents his own slant on the meeting. Clark noticed that von Senger spoke in 'perfect Oxford English' when they met. The Americans had removed their sidearms, and as von Senger left to read the terms of the surrender a journalist pointed out that the general was wearing a small sidearm across his back. Von Senger was called back, and Clark described 'that very stiffly, his face expressionless, von Senger took off the leather belt and let the gun holster swing downward. Very stiffly, he swung it toward the foot of the tree outside the shack and turned away as it thumped softly against the ground', and Clark had it picked up to keep as a souvenir.[11] When together Clark recorded that they had a brief discussion on some of the past battles. Clark wondered why they were not fully attacked at Salerno, and von Senger replied that Kesselring thought it might be a feint to cover for another landing further up the coast. Clark asked why they stayed south of the Po, and von Senger simply replied 'Hitler' as if, Clark noted, that this explained everything, which for von Senger it did.[12]

Clark had the Germans' meeting building fully bugged so they could hear everything, and because there was little to report he sent them some whisky. They overheard the Germans talking of the possibility that Hitler would commit suicide and Clark thought the whisky had worked.[13] However, Clark recalled that they were 'cooperative in carrying out the surrender details', but noted that many Germans were deserting and heading north, and according to him von Senger claimed they wanted to avoid Italian insults by making their way home and were worried about the partisans, which also reflected von Senger's memories.[14]

It soon became clear the German presence was no longer required and on 13 May von Senger and his staff were flown back to Bolzano, and he returned to his old headquarters. A week later on 22 May with his adjutant Count von Cramm they were taken into captivity, and he was sent as a leader of a huge PoW camp at Ghedi (a town in the province of Brescia in Lombardy). This tented prison camp was situated on the airport with von Senger estimating at least 100,000 inmates. He had to make immediate adjustments knowing he had no authority, having stopped in his command of fighting at a place of sheer impotence. He was now seen as a soldier of a hated regime and cut off from his family and the outside world. Amongst the officers and soldiers, he felt they treated him as part of the problem, as men in his position as one-time generals were seen as responsible for leading everyone to their current situation. He talked to the men but noted their indifference, and the one relief he felt was that he was no longer in the position of feeling he had to tell lies. He also felt good about being free of the Nazi regime though he quickly gathered many in the camp did not recognise this freedom.

He was not there long as the writer Klaus Mann (son of Thomas Mann) had written in the American Army newspaper (*Stars and Stripes*) that the man in charge at Ghedi was a German general and not American commander. The intention had been to take him to Modena, but the intended officers' camp was not yet built, so he was put into a German rest camp which had been surrounded with barbed wire and given his own large tent. He was told he would be going elsewhere, and then finally into the officers' camp where he was pleased to find some sharing of his own views within discussion groups. He had only just settled in when he was told he and some other generals would be taken to a camp at Aversa just north of Naples. He recalled passing the scarred battlefields of Cassino but now at peace. The new camp was something of a disappointment which consisted of many types of barrack buildings surrounded by barbed wire which no one could cross. They passed the time by learning languages, reading, and arranging discussion groups, from which it may be assumed von Senger found some people like himself. They rarely saw American officers so were unable to make any form of requests, and they were ordered to salute American officers if they saw them, but who were not allowed to return the salute; it was indicative of organised contempt, though some American officers did respond. The contempt for German prisoners was growing rife because the news of the barbaric concentration camps was becoming public and widely broadcast. This reaction to the Holocaust and other ethnic massacres was seen as a form of corporate responsibility that every German had to carry. Such was the disgust for many on the Allied side, it seemed to justify the immense carpet-bombing raids, and it was always assumed the senior German officers must have known about the camps. There is no doubt that most Germans had heard of the camps, Dachau Concentration Camp was set up as early as March 1933, and initially used as a place to intimidate or kill those Germans who opposed the Nazi Party. It is likely that rumours abounded, but it is now clear the barbarities of the extermination camps came as a shock to many. It was all too natural for the Allies to assume that because a person was a high-up general, he must have known these appalling details.

This was the time when some senior officers and others were being brought to trial for war crimes, and one of them asked for von Senger's help because of his linguistic skills. Von Senger agreed, but pointed out he had no judicial training, though once had set off to study law until war started in 1914. However, those not facing prosecution were decamped and sent north (now late 1945) and from the train walked over a mile to the new camp near Heilbronn (a city in northern Baden-Württemberg, Germany). On arrival some 30 of them were ushered into a large tent which was leaking. Next, they were moved to a prison in Hall where two shared a cell. Von Senger must have felt as if he were on a tortuous trek as he was taken by himself to the prison in Heidelberg, no companions and no reasons appeared to signify the orders of the day. A few days later he was taken to the airport where a two-seater aircraft was to take him back to Italy. Von Senger found the pilot did not know the way and was short of fuel. They landed at Marseilles where his officer escort gave him a much-needed meal. The pilot, concerned about fuel, flew over Corsica and into Rome. This journey was all to do with his friend General Dostler. The next day, after a pleasant conversation with the pilot they flew into Aversa where Dostler was held. Dostler regarded von Senger as a good colleague and had requested his help, which von Senger could only do when the defence counsel was present. Not long afterwards they were moved to Rome where the trial would be held. Von Senger was being regarded as an authority on the conditions within the Wehrmacht and felt he was treated in the same way as the accused. There were courtroom debates as to the validity of the trial, it had not been authorised by Field Marshal Alexander but by a subordinate American general, but the protests failed, and the trial proceeded. The trial focused on the evidence that Dostler had conformed with Hitler's directive (19 October 1942) that commandos or saboteurs were to be executed, in this particular case the incident was generally known by its code, the Giny Mission. Von Senger accepted that Hitler's orders were criminal, but that Dostler had no choice but to obey his orders. This was a crunch-line debate in the Nuremberg Trials where obeying criminal and immoral orders was deemed as wrong. Von Senger was pleased with himself when he raised the point that in North Africa an Allied commander ordered a commando unit not to take prisoners. He may have had another embarrassing argument for the prosecution, had he known then that General George Patton had ignored two incidents when some of his soldiers twice massacred groups of Italian prisoners. The old legal argument of *tu quoque* (you did the same) was ignored in the Dostler trial as it was at Nuremberg. The defence counsel even raised the point that American high command expected orders to be obeyed. It was raised that the SD had arrived to take the prisoners, but Dostler had refused them, possibly with the intention of not having them killed. Dostler was sentenced to death by firing squad and von Senger visited him beforehand, too sad and upset to say anything.

Later, long after von Senger had died, an American history researcher discovered that Dostler at the time of the decision was in the company of Kesselring which cast murkier shadows over the much-respected Field Marshal. When it came to Kesselring's trial, he had realised the shooting of hostages was more in the grey area of international law than killing PoWs. Kesselring's own counsel, Laternser had already underlined this point establishing that when ex-PoWs had been caught with the partisans, they were still treated as PoWs. Kesselring knew the Allied courts showed no leniency in matters of killing PoWs. In his estimation it was safer to be tried for massacring 335 Italian people (Ardeatine Cave massacre) than fifteen American soldiers. The American history researcher, Richard Raiber produced evidence which, while not conclusive, is persuasive. He found evidence that the knowledge of the raid, the Ginny mission, was 'known to Kesselring's HQ', and Kesselring was with Dostler and not at Monte Cassino.[15] Dostler, a pro-Hitler general, always claimed the order to execute was confirmed from above, and Dostler claimed that Kesselring's HQ had asked whether it had been done, which conflicts with both Kesselring's and Westphal's testimony. Significantly an Ultra intercept to Kesselring's HQ announced that the Americans had been liquidated.[16] A reserve cavalry captain, Alexander Fürst zu Dohna-Schlobitten, noted in his diary his refusal to shoot the PoWs, observing they were regarded as saboteurs. In his autobiography von Senger postulated that Dostler would have received authorisation from HQ, and he found it strange that Dostler's chief of staff could not be located, even though he was a PoW.[17] Von Senger also admitted to the court that Hitler 'gave out orders which in their way interfered with International Law'.[18]

The written evidence remained evasive until Raiber checked telephone logs, and discovered Westphal noting that on the date he claimed to be at Cassino, Kesselring 'was still up in North Italy...complaining that the defences at Genoa are much too weak'.[19] Another document relating to Kesselring's itinerary shows that he arrived at an airfield north of Genoa, and was 'met by Dostler'.[20] This was further substantiated by entries in the war diaries of 'Sea Commandant, Italian Riviera and the German Navy Command, Italy'.[21] The Ginny Americans had been moved to La Spezia at the same time Kesselring was there. The lack of written evidence was, as confirmed later by several German officers, because all records regarding the Ginny mission were destroyed, by order from Monte Soratte, Kesselring's HQ. It would appear from this research that Kesselring, Westphal and others were in cahoots, but it was not until 1997 that Beelitz 'admitted Kesselring had been in Liguria on 24 March 1944'.[22] Dostler probably kept quiet because of *Korpsgeist* (*esprit de corps*), knowing he was going to die anyway. Raiber hoped there might be evidence in the Ultra intercepts in London, but after an examination of some 300 such intercepts this research found nothing.

Raiber's work and later admissions indicate that Kesselring and his officers were in cahoots at the trial, and deliberately lied on the grounds that they knew it would be fatal to be associated with the killing of American prisoners. What Raiber never raised was the critical question as to the attitudes of the day, that it was considered safer to be tried for the death of 335 innocent Italians than fifteen American soldiers. The Italians had initially been the enemy, but the massacre of innocent civilians could not be regarded as less serious than shooting PoWs. It has been suggested that 'one of the peculiarities of that postwar period was that Allied officers felt an admiration for their German counterparts regardless of their criminal and unmilitary activities, so long as the victims were not British or American'.[23] The Wehrmacht's behaviour to civilians was atrocious, but killing PoWs was by law and attitude regarded as more serious, by both sides.

Von Senger had always admired Kesselring even if at times he disagreed with him, and this information would have shocked him. Von Senger would have known that Kesselring was condemned to death, that it was commuted to a life sentence. This was because the Western alliance was trying to ensure West Germany was onside against the Soviet threat, and they released Kesselring and many other senior figures from prison. Von Senger would also have known that Kesselring persisted in stubbornly remaining a strong right-winger, was never critical about Hitler, and was at times an embarrassment to the new postwar German government which von Senger would later willingly serve.

After the trial von Senger was moved back to the Aversa PoW camp and a few weeks later sent to a British camp at Afragola, near Naples. This camp was unpleasant, they had to remove their trousers at night and sleep on the bare ground. Next day von Senger complained and said he had attended the trial as a witness and not a criminal. This protest worked and after a few enquiries he was transferred to an ordinary officers' camp. Each one had his own tent, but it was not helped by the weather turning bitterly cold. Von Senger found it bemusing that the only SS officer had been placed in charge, but at least he was polite and correct. Time seemed endless and dragged, but von Senger admitted they were fortunate enough not to have fallen into Soviet arms, many who did remain prisoners long after the war. He was in the camp some three months and fell ill, but recovered quickly when he slept on a hospital mattress. He recalled being visited by a British sergeant who was very pleasant, and one day was taken by surprise when he was escorted to the gates. He found he was being visited by friends, the Bishop of Veroli and the Campanari family bringing him cakes, as well as a gift from the Benedictine nuns at Veroli. He did not mention the reaction of the guards who must have been bemused to find a German general being visited by an Italian bishop. He was also joined by two ex-comrades Vietinghoff and Lemelsen who had come from a PoW camp in Rimini where the conditions were much better. The next morning, they all took a flight. Von Senger later discovered that his 19-year-old daughter had travelled in a Red Cross truck all the way through Italy to try and find him. When writing his account, he was understandably pleased he did not know this at the time. This time he was on the way to Britain. His first stop was at the London Cage, where contrary to many statements about this site in Kensington, he felt well-treated. They were questioned about war crimes in their area, and von Senger was able to prove he had often refused top directives about summary executions, and his views on the subject were accepted.

After two weeks in the Cage (where Kesselring had been and made a life-long friend of the officer in charge, a Colonel Scotland), and having established he was not a potential war criminal he was transferred to a PoW camp for high-ranking officers at Bridgend in South Wales, including Field Marshals Brauchitsch, Manstein, and Rundstedt. Interestingly, very much as General Paulus had discovered in the Soviet prison camps, the prisoners remained divided over loyalty to the Führer and the Nazi regime. Von Senger's group tended to be those wanting to clear up the past and were generally opposed to Nazism and had felt this during most of the war. There was a second group which had started to change their minds following the consequences of defeat, and the third type who remained stubbornly supportive of the swastika. Naturally there was tension between the first group and the others if not hostility, which paralleled Paulus' experience in Soviet Russia.

In Russia the Soviets tried to indoctrinate, with some success, by bringing in left-wing Germans to try and reason with them. Paulus was told he would be meeting some Germans who wanted to speak with him. One would be Wilhelm Pieck, who like Walter Ulbricht had once been a member of the German Reichstag.* Pieck was well informed and communicative, telling Paulus the current disaster would never have happened had he and the German people not allowed themselves to be misled by Hitler. Paulus could only reply that he could not believe that the head of state would betray his people, and he was only doing his duty. There is little doubt that these questions started to have an effect on Paulus once he realised what was happening to his homeland of Germany.

In Britain they brought in some German emigrants to join the discussions, and von Senger noted they were listened to, but there was not much dialogue. Most of the inmates were wondering how long they would be held prisoner, some angry about the detention, all worried about their families in Germany, and a few were concerned about being indicted on war crimes. Von Senger found it difficult to cope with the pro-Nazis often putting it down to a poor education, which today still makes sense. He tried to persuade some to reconsider their views, and discovered their knowledge was badly limited. He stood back as it dawned on him that the more knowledgeable ones bore more responsibility than those who were ignorant, thereby supporting the Nazi regime simply because it was the government. He also pondered why some nations had experienced successful dictatorship and seemed to have flourished even though they allowed no political freedom, which on this writer's reflection, was still far from offering any real hope. In terms of those who accepted Nazism he simply could not understand why, writing that 'in this respect the average Army general had been like all other citizens except that he embodied

* He would later be chairman of the Socialist Unity Party from 1946 to 1950, and then president of the GDR between 1949 to 1960.

these weaknesses to a higher degree'.[24] He added that in Germany many people tended to adopt the political views of the military. This was a curious view to offer given that many military leaders, including Kesselring, were constantly arguing they held no military views, as their role was simply to obey the government. This was of course a highly suspect claim in itself, but it was a common claim stemming from the Prussian dogma of obedience. He was right in so far that most military are expected to obey, but whether they would have agreed to massacring ethnic groups raises more than a few eyebrows. It is known that von Senger refused such commands, but he could only speak for himself and not try and whitewash every German military commander. In Britain, it was known that some bomber crew members suddenly felt revolted by indiscriminate mass-bombing, and they refused to keep flying on such missions. They had their dismissal cards stamped LMF (Lack of Moral Fibre) and were sent elsewhere; in Nazi Germany the response would have been very different. Von Senger noticed that many had failed to note the weakness if not the moral ineptitude of the German political leaders of the time, which he had, but accepted their overall policies of invading other countries, even if he did not obey the more immoral and criminal orders. He noted that some had justifiably reproached the generals because their opposition only emerged when it eventually dawned on them that Hitler's war instructions were leading to failure. He noted that it was often Christian generals who developed some form of resistance, whether Protestant or Catholic, and although he was undoubtedly correct some critics might point out given the unprecedented barbarity, the resistance was not strong enough. However, it was a deeply complex area which for von Senger meant a degree of compassion for his comrades, which was understandable.

In the Bridgend camp he was appointed to be the camp's Press Officer, which gave him the opportunity to read the British weeklies and even some of their daily press. He felt this way he was able to exert a degree of education for the prisoners, especially by underlining the political issues. He was also able to demonstrate for them the way Germany had estranged itself from the rest of the world, writing that 'nor did I conceal from my audience that one of the first to subscribe to the relief of the hungry population of Germany was the Jewish publisher Gollancz'.[25]

That Germany was regarded not just as a pariah state but as unliked and causing suspicion was widely prevalent for many years. This writer was born on Holocaust Day in 1945, and he can recall even in the 1950s that the Germans were still regarded by many as the enemy.

It was, von Senger rightly decided, necessary to find a way back to essential moral standards of law, order, and civic life to live within the community of nations. He recorded that at Bridgend they had two British commandants, who both epitomised the British gentleman in so far that they were polite, courteous, and sympathetic to the prisoners. He and a few other prisoners were allowed to walk out of the prison boundaries and take a stroll without a guard around the country estate, and they also had sufficient food. They worked as gardeners in the estate dominated by a large house. The camp had been known as Island Farm and had been well-known for the largest escape attempt by German prisoners during the war. As the war ended it was renamed Special Camp XI to detain many prisoners including SS awaiting extradition to stand trial in Nuremberg and elsewhere. It was also used to incarcerate captured German generals from the most senior to lesser-known generals such as von Senger.

Von Senger worked with a couple of others in the garden, but he was soon the only German there. He noted the owner of the estate was reserved, not just with von Senger but with everyone, and as far as von Senger could see he never went hunting and had a beautiful young wife who even brought him cake on occasions. When there was a hunt meeting in the locality the wife said von Senger could attend, the camp commandant agreed, and von Senger followed the pack on foot, though compared to what he was accustomed to did not think it was of the highest order. On Sundays they were given more liberty and allowed to attend the church of their choice, with von Senger attending Mass with the Roman Catholics. The camp was visited by different denominations including the Plymouth Brethren. The various groups brought cakes with them and discussed their faith. He found the Anglicans, Methodists, and Baptists more moderate, visiting but not trying to convert. Von Senger was obviously trusted because the Lutherans were unhappy about their own German pastor. They asked von Senger to give his opinion of their spiritual leader. He interceded on their behalf, but they continued to shun their pastor, who thereafter often visited von Senger in his cell. The German protestants found the Church of England too Catholic for their liking, which bemused von Senger as he knew the Church of England had a wide spectrum, mentioning the High Church, which was more Catholic than the Low Church, which was more like the German Lutheran. Von Senger provided one interesting insight, namely the lack of division between the denominations, which he believed had arisen from the previous years with the need for people to stand together.

The only unhappy note he found was that he was limited in the number of lines he could write to his wife once a month. He knew she felt lonely in Göttingen, but he was pleased to hear that the British Commandant in their hometown was kind, had visited her, and the Commandant's wife had exchanged provisions with her. She managed with others to make ends meet by selling antiques to American soldiers, and he was pleased that in her earlier life she had been keen on collecting such items. His old college of St Johns in Oxford heard of his captivity and tried to arrange for his son to pay a visit, but this failed because of the 'bureaucratic machinery'. Before his son arrived in Oxford von Senger had been repatriated, but the President of the College befriended him, and von Senger would often spend time ruminating on his wonderful experience at Oxford.

The camp was also visited by Captain B. H. Liddell Hart, today still respected as a military historian. Von Senger recognised that unlike many, Liddell Hart was well disposed towards the Germans, and after captivity they became good friends both professionally and personally. He met Liddell Hart in his home, and von Senger was visited by him in Germany the day the Korean War started. In the Liddell Hart archives at King's College, London, are many letters and papers indicating that von Senger and Liddell Hart stayed in constant touch and friendship, which also included von Senger's son Ferdinand who became a general in the new West Germany, and this friendship included even von Senger's wife Hilda.[26] Liddell Hart mentioned von Senger's son Ferdinand several times in his book *The Other Side of the Hill*, not least his knowledge about Russian tank building.[27] This reference to the work of a captain at the time was probably because of his friendship with von Senger his friend. He mentions von Senger as commanding the forces in Sicily, which was something of an exaggeration, but rightly commends him for the evacuation of forces from Corsica and Sardinia.[28] The papers in the archives include newspaper cuttings, discussions on tank tactics, and notes on a BBC television broadcast von Senger later gave. It was evident that Liddell Hart in his research into German tactics used von Senger's inside knowledge, discussing with him the work of the German High Command (OKW), the operations in Sicily and even Russian tank development.[29] It was both a professional and a personal relationship which developed from the meeting in the prison camp.

He was also visited by an old Oxford friend Kurt Hahn. This German friend had a strong character, he was raised Jewish and spoke out against Hitler and was duly imprisoned. He was a well-known educator who founded schools in Germany, but due to the intervention of Prime Minister Ramsay MacDonald he was able to escape the Nazi clutches, and he moved to Britain. He settled in Scotland and founded Gordonstoun School (which British royalty later attended, namely Prince Philip and the current King Charles III) on the same strict principles as his well-known Salem School in Germany. He converted to Christianity in the Church of England and by 1945 was preaching in the Church of Scotland. Later he was involved in founding and assisting the Outward-Bound Course, Atlantic College, and the Duke of Edinburgh's Award scheme. This friendship with Hahn clearly indicated that von Senger was respected for his integrity and intellect, these two elements not always coming together. Hahn suggested to von Senger he could teach in one of his schools, which he did for a brief time in Germany at the Salem School.

Not long after this visit by Hahn, when returning to camp, it was the sentry who broke the news, congratulating him on his release. Von Senger and others travelled on 13 May 1948 through Oxford to Newmarket to the dispersal camp at Bury St Edmunds, embarking at Harwich for the Netherlands. The British Commandant had accompanied them throughout the journey and drove him and two others to Hanover.

Von Senger knew he was returning to a country where there were raging debates about the past, and that his own home had become a billet for many with his wife reduced to one room. He arrived late at night: 'very quietly I stepped into the garden behind the house and gave the low whistle that was our special signal. P [his wife] appeared on the veranda', thus concluding his war memoirs.[30]

Von Senger's Views of the War Years

In the final pages of his memoirs, he pauses during the various stages and in his typical style writes in detail about the war, revealing once again an intellectual and astute mind with an analysis of both sides of the great divide. He did not write this until he was finishing the book in the late 1950s, as many of his insights, which few modern historians would quarrel with would have been gleaned postwar. The next few pages will not be detailed, but they are mentioned to indicate where his mind was focused. He explored Britain's planning organisation, studying the way the three services worked together under the Chiefs of Staff led by Alan Brooke of the Army, Portal for the RAF and then first Pound then Cunningham for the Royal Navy. He knew Churchill often had fantastic ideas (which Brooke often described in his diaries as mad) and that the service chiefs were able to keep this under control. He also noted the military services were able to act in a coordinated fashion. He was a great admirer of General (Pug) Ismay, Churchill's Chief of Staff, writing that his influence was 'actually greater than that of any Minister outside the Cabinet'. In stating this he was exaggerating Ismay's importance, as Pug Ismay was better known for his loyalty to Churchill, his friendly good nature, and the hard work he did during and after the war.

He noted the American system was different, as the President's role included being Commander-in-Chief of the armed forces. However, he noted that Churchill probably carried more influence over the British armed forces. The President relied heavily upon General George Marshall and Admiral King, (the American Air Force was part of the Army) and he tended to give his Chiefs of Staff full authority. The American and British Staffs worked together, mainly in Washington with Field Marshal Sir John Dill as the liaison officer for the British, whom von Senger had admired before the war when they had met. He knew there had been friction between the two allies and moments of extreme tension at most meetings, most of it based on different views regarding strategy. The Americans could not understand why the British were so keen to fight in

Africa, then invade Sicily and the Italian mainland. They wanted to cross the channel and head for Berlin. What von Senger did not know was that Brooke, the British Chief of the Imperial General Staff (CIGS) persuaded them to delay the cross-channel invasion until they were better prepared. The American General Omar Bradley in his memoirs wrote, 'I came to the conclusion that it was fortunate that the British view prevailed, that the US Army first met the enemy on the periphery, in Africa rather than on the beaches of France. In Africa we learnt to crawl, to walk and then run. Had that learning process been launched in France it would surely have, as Alan Brooke argued, resulted in an unthinkable disaster'.[31] The clashes continued over the British not being in favour of the invasion of southern France, but the Americans were now the major partner.

Von Senger also looked at the work of the supreme commanders in the different theatres of the war across the globe. He noted the weakness of the American command structure when during the Korean War there was outright conflict between the politically elected President and the military Commander General MacArthur. In his own experience of the Second World War, von Senger noted the various changes in command, but he noted that the Americans carried the most resources and were therefore the major influence. He did not mention that the German Nazi politicians had completely underestimated the industrial strength of the USA.

He then moved onto the strategic controversies between the Allies, not least noting the differences between and the Eastern and Western Fronts, with different rules prevailing. He noticed the pressure for a second front which Stalin was constantly demanding, but less so once the Russians turned the tide against Germany. He noted there was always the potential of east-west tensions becoming serious, giving the forlorn hope to some misguided Nazis that the West might join them in the fight against Bolshevism. He noted that both Roosevelt and Stalin were unhappy with Churchill's insistence to finish the war in Italy before giving the troops over for invading France. Churchill's argument was for tying down German forces, supported by Alexander who in his memoirs wrote that 'it was the Germans, not the Allies, who were contained in Italy'.[32] However, years later he once said during an interview he was never sure who was tying down who.

Von Senger almost revels in his analysis of pointing out the battlefield controversies, not least the time the American General Mark Clark deliberately took Rome instead of entrapping the German 10th Army at Valmonte, and the controversies over Operation *Anvil*, later *Dragoon* (South France invasion) taking so much time and tension. He referred to the strained relationships between Montgomery and Eisenhower over the nature of the attack on Germany having taken France. Montgomery wanted a single broad thrust to Berlin whereas Eisenhower wanted a long broad front. Von Senger thought Montgomery's idea was better and closer to German military policy, but it could be argued that Eisenhower's plan was safer and would cost less lives. Von Senger may have agreed to this when he then noted that after Stalingrad the Germans should have sought some form of peace or at least capitulated. He also recognised the fact that Hitler's Ardennes offensive [commonly known as the Battle of the Bulge] was nothing more than 'the last spurt of a mortally wounded combatant'.

Von Senger noted that the German failure had led to the domination and threat of the Soviet Union and wrote that it was only Churchill who had foreseen this probability. Von Senger finally turned his attention to the cause of defeat of Germany, using a very broad sweep of his brush. He started with the world's political developments. Germany had a history of being tuned into central Europe, and Von Senger noted Alexis de Tocqueville, a nineteenth century French historian, who had once claimed that there could only be two world powers, namely Russia and America, whereas Germany was busy establishing its national unity by a series of local wars, not interested in colonial enterprise, and became engulfed in their perception of the 'encirclement complex', namely surrounded by potential enemies. Von Senger noted that in both world wars Germany over-calculated her strength, and they landed up fighting what almost amounted to a worldwide coalition.

Von Senger pointed out the internal political strife resulting in a dictatorship and the 'graveyard stillness' caused by a dominant police state. None of this was helped, von Senger added, by having a psychopathic leader whose henchmen were of the same breed, a sickness that infected some of the Wehrmacht. Von Senger commented on the Prussian military traditions and noted that some of these military commanders found Hitler odious because of his proletarian tendencies. To the modern reader this social classification may sound like nonsense when they should have been looking to a leader with some form of moral values. He also pointed out a few more principled commanders like Beck who had seen the dangers in the Nazi foreign policy and stepped back. As somc resigned or objected to Hitler's ideas they were soon replaced by officers, who either by indoctrination or wishing to enhance their career projectile, gave their total cooperation. The Prussian military image left its mark on most of Germany, but von Senger does not make much of an issue of the accepted rules of blind obedience which would be raised at the Nuremberg trial. He also noted that Germany was a land power and was fighting sea power nations. It had been the blockade of Germany in the First World War which had created so many serious problems. Despite the U-boat warfare in the Atlantic, America was able to send supplies both to Britain and – helped by the Royal Navy – supplies into Russia. Von Senger also noted that Russia had been underestimated in terms of both its manpower and its potential industrial output, which became more than clear with their massive supplies of tanks. It took time for the senior military staff to realise that in the circumstances of a major world war it could not be done by clever and large outflanking battles, which belonged more to the time of Napoleon.

Because of Germany's landlocked situation resources were often short, which affected, von Senger noted, the morale of the fighting men, which was clearly seen at the Battle of Stalingrad. He noted that the cause of the military failure was not just political or military but psychological. The Nazi Party (NSDAP) had made promises of a better future, better life, but with no talk of genocide and war, and with their homes being blown apart as well as their family lives, attitudes had changed. He noted that those with a religious background found the regime was trying to replace it with their own pseudo-philosophy.

Curiously, von Senger noted that even the more intelligent and educated people had seen the weaknesses of the Weimar democracy and had approved of a firm leadership, and Hitler's early successes had seemed to confirm this aspect. The economic growth appeared good even if it were a preparation for war. There was more money, but few noticed the government simply printed more, and it helped conceal the internal economic regeneration as the 1936 Olympics tended to blind the outside world. He offered in his study, many reasons for the failure, but he does not raise the sheer barbarity of the regime epitomised by the Holocaust which stirred up an anger at Germany, with many Allied soldiers on seeing the camps now feeling why the war had to be fought. He noted, as well as elsewhere in his memoirs that effective opposition to the Nazi regime had been impossible, and asked the question in his final paragraph as to 'how could so many Germans shut their eyes to all these wretched aberrations and crimes?'[33]

Von Senger, who as previously noted, first met Liddell Hart the soldier and military historian while a prisoner at Bridgend PoW camp, and they had become close friends with Liddell Hart writing the preface to von Senger's study, describing it as one of the best war memoirs ever written. He wrote that it shed light not only on the tactics, but the battlefield conditions. He also proposed that it was written by a traditional German who found himself working for the Nazi regime. Liddell Hart found that von Senger was more open to admitting the errors and the evils than most of his contemporaries. He also made the point that von Senger made every effort to be as objective as possible, and his analysis of the war in terms of political and military control, of strategy and tactics, of tensions between Allies, few modern historians could disagree (with a few probably wanting a tweak here and there).

Chapter 6

Postwar Years

Von Senger's life after he was released and returned home was a matter, for once, of being recognised as a person with value and much to offer, but this chapter need only be a summary. He was always a private man in his own writings, rarely referring to his family by name, and in his war-memoirs referring to his wife Hilda as 'P'. He became involved in education as his initial occupation on release, but his help was enlisted by the new Bonn West German government on some military matters. It must have been a very strange twist of fate in a life which since 1914 had been involved in the military, the latter years of the Second World War fraught with battle and serious decision making. He had felt obliged to work for a regime he detested, and which clashed with both his religious, intellectual, and moral leanings. He always remained a junior general, but despite his lowly position in the higher rankings, he was highly respected by many on both sides of the great divide, and he was obviously liked because of his personality. Much of what is known about his life comes from the Italian historian Giuseppe Trulli who managed to find out some information from remaining family members.[1] Von Senger knew he was returning to a beloved wife with their family torn apart by the war, and that their home had been taken over by what appeared to be a series of billeted residents. Quite possibly because of his old Oxford friend Kurt Hahn visiting him in Bridgend PoW Camp, the idea of teaching for a new living had entered his head. As such he became the headmaster (some claim housemaster) of the Spetzgart school near Überlingen (Salem) on Lake Constance, a school very much associated with Kurt Hahn. He was not exactly overwhelmed by his new work which would not have been surprising after the previous ten years in the army. He really needed a sense of peace, free of the horrors of the past, having served a regime which he detested, and wanted the solitude to write his memoirs of those fraught and disturbing years. The regime had left him totally disillusioned and unhappy that the traditional Germany he had loved was now divided between the four victors including the Soviet form of Bolshevism, a government he had always seen as potentially dangerous. He was also very aware that Germany's reputation on an international basis was in tatters after the disclosures at the Nuremberg Trials, and the following worldwide publicity which made Germany a pariah state which would take time to restore. It is clear from his views that von Senger was no rampant nationalist, his time at Oxford, his vast linguistic abilities had made him aware of other countries and their values, and he frequently referred to the 'community of nations'. He was, like so many, patriotic, and it was understandable that he found the changes postwar sad and depressing in his home country.

Even when involved in the battles he had found time to wander into the countryside to the loneliest of places to be by himself surrounded by nature and beautiful scenery. Given this aspect of his nature, it was not surprising that he purchased a small farmhouse in the rural village of Häg-Happach. It was deep in the Black Forest set on a rock at a high altitude of nearly 3,000 feet. He and his wife were isolated in this new home but within easy driving distance of Basel. It was a place where he could enjoy family life, meet close friends, and it was here he found the time and peace to reflect on writing his memoirs. Some of his correspondence noted by Trulli indicates he stayed in touch with his friend Campanari with whom he once billeted in Italy, sent his greetings to the various Italian clergy he had met. This postwar correspondence clearly indicated his pleasant nature, because he had billeted in Campanari's home, and they had stayed good friends long after the war. Many such people may well have been polite having a German general billeted on them, but because of von Senger's open nature many of these friendships lasted to his death. He spent much time in his home writing his memoirs which he entitled *Krieg in Europa* (War in Europe) as well as other works on military theory.

As noted, he was very much aware that after the war Germany needed both internal and external reconstructing, a form of healing process. People knew his feelings and he was invited to attend the Königswinter conference led by Lilo Milchsack. She was a lady determined to work for healing the relationships between Britain and Germany, often claimed to be one of the main constructors of postwar Europe. It was at this congress he met and worked with the future German President Richard von Weizsäcker and other major German politicians, and also met British politicians Denis Healey, Richard Crossman, and the well-known journalist Robin Day.

In 1950 he was one of many ex-military generals who were trusted by the new government to work on the Himmerod Memorandum. This was intended to address the question of West Germany's (Federal Republic of Germany) rearmament and was organised by Chancellor Konrad Adenauer, called Himmerod because the gathering met in the Himmerod Abbey. It established a new military force known as the *Bundeswehr*. The West German Allied military commanders welcomed this because of the rising fears of the Cold War, and they referred to the old Wehrmacht's 'honour' which raised dubious hopes they had fought a clean war. Von Senger and a few others had tried, but not all generals and men had fought a so-called clean war. There were still old right-wing generals slowly emerging from incarceration such as Kesselring who could see no reason for a new name, preferring Wehrmacht. As the Second World War had raged the Allies had agreed that when Germany was defeated it would have no military, be denazified, decentralised and made democratic. The growth of the Cold War was now creating a change of attitude in the West who need their parts of Germany onside. Many of the Himmerod conference expected that for the *Bundeswehr* to be successful certain drastic steps had to be taken. These including releasing German soldiers convicted of war crimes (which included Kesselring) and that the defamation of the Wehrmacht soldier and Waffen-SS had to stop, all of which Konrad Adenauer accepted before negotiating with the Allies. There were many commanders in attendance including von Senger's old acquaintance von Vietinghoff.

There were many outside the governmental and military circles who were becoming not only suspicious but critical of these developments, namely inviting ex-Nazi generals for assistance. One famous German diarist, Victor Klemperer, a Jewish academic who survived the war but was now still in his home city of Dresden (part of Soviet Eastern Germany), was beginning to become critical of the Soviet rule which he dubbed the Fourth Reich. In his third diary he also kept a beady eye on the rumours circulating from the Western zone.[2] He had become alert when in 1949 Adenauer had denounced the denazification process pursued by the Allies, and in 1951 demanded an end to '*sniffing out Nazis*', which undoubtedly benefited many but would not have pleased Klemperer, who had experienced the suffering created by Nazism. In 1956 his core instinct was against Bonn with its 'Jew-murderer ministers', initiated by the end of denazification in the West. In August 1957 he wrote of the constant chatter about morality and lies, and 'at the moment things are evidently more brutal, more Asiatic here than in the Adenauer state. But over there is the most blatant return to Nazism – here to Bolshevism'. His cynicism was probably understandable, he may have been more relaxed with a man like von Senger, but it must have felt like an unwelcome blast from the past.

Von Senger would have been proud of his son Ferdinand who became a General within the *Bundeswehr* and later a well-known military author, and von Senger himself became more and more busy with the new government spending up to three or four days in Bonn. They were seeking his military experience and knowledge of military life to find the best possible officers for the new *Bundeswehr*, and this kept him occupied from 1954 for many years. Amongst a myriad of tasks, he became a military correspondent for the Südwestfunk Broadcasting organisation, somewhat cautious about the NATO rearming, but from 1952 in a fairly secret capacity served as a consultant for the Adenauer government.

He was constantly in and out of Bonn, with even some scientific societies requiring his presence, and chased by publishers who wanted to publish the work they gathered he was working on. In 1956 he was still going to Bonn to advise on the selection of senior officers, and also made busy in Karlsruhe helping the Americans on their version and compilation of the history of the war.

This work with the Americans was interesting and included his appraisal of the situation in Italy, entitled *Liaison Activities with Italian 6th Army – A Postwar study by General von Senger und Etterlin, with Comments by Generals Halder and Mueller-Hillebrand.*[3] On reading this account it soon became clear that this work was either used as part of his memoirs, or the memoirs were well underway, and he was using them for American consumption. It was also interesting to note that both Generals Mueller-Hillebrand and Franz Halder were critical of Von Senger's work. The former praised him for his careful consideration but passing generalised assessments beyond the sphere of his experience. Halder was more critical, accepting that von Senger had utilised the official war diary, but again stating some of the generalisations he was not equipped to make. They both seemed to overlook that von Senger was presenting the picture from an historical point of view and looking at the situation, as always, from the political angle, which Halder dismissed as 'carrying coals to Newcastle'. Von Senger also produced for the Americans the *War Diary of the Italian Campaign* which is referred to in the end notes and primary sources as C-095, and which was already either part of his developing memoirs, or he used the same notes as the basis for his personal work, but it is clear that his opinions remained firm and consistent.

This led him in the same year to go to the USA to give a lecture at various military academies, and later repeating this trip in 1957 to lecture at some classes at the Air Force Colonels School. He never explained what the lectures were about, but it is not difficult to speculate that it was probably a mixture of the importance of air power from which he and his troops had suffered, the nature of defence in the Italian terrain of which he would have been regarded as an experienced expert. Later Kesselring would be quizzed on fighting the Allies as well as the partisans, and von Senger may have had to deal with this as well, as the Americans were keen to learn about this difficult subject.

In 1958 he went on a visit to Paris with NATO officers, who were giving lectures under his presidency. It was clear that despite once being a German and therefore Nazi General he was respected not just because of his experience, but his moral views and sociability were obviously apparent. In 1960 he was interviewed on BBC television *Face to Face* and was also part of a BBC radio discussion on the Battle at Monte Cassino.

It was by this year he was beginning to feel his age, which given he was virtually 70 years old was not surprising. He was not able to walk up mountains and steep hills anymore but remained intellectually alert and desperate to finish his book. Despite ill health caused by heart problems, he continued to work, giving lectures in Paris, London, Oxford, and back in Bologna, but needed Hilda to prepare the trips and even carry his cases. He was falling ill but not slowing down, and on 4 January 1963 he died in Freiburg. He was buried in Häg graveyard, and his wife Hilda joined him twenty year later in 1983.

Chapter 7

Final Observations

The questions surrounding von Senger vary, but the main one tends to be the trustworthiness of his memoirs. Whether they fell into the category of postwar justification by standing apart from the Nazi regime, or whether he had these feelings and attitudes during the war years. Even his main opponent on the battlefield, General Mark Clark, described von Senger as an Anglophile known for his anti-Nazi attitudes, claiming this was the reason his outstanding defence of Cassino was played done by the authorities. There is considerable evidence from the war and postwar years that the memoirs are generally honest and reflect their author. There are four issues worth focusing on starting with why he fought for a regime he despised, his politics in general, what he offered as a military commander, and finally the man von Senger himself.

Fighting for Hitler

In Shakespeare's play *Henry V* in Act IV Scene I, the king in disguise wanders amongst his soldiers so they do not recognise him and can speak their mind to him, believing him to be just another soldier on the eve of a battle. When Henry was asked who he was, he explained he was just serving under Sir Thomas Erpingham and raised the question that they are fighting for a 'just and honourable cause'. A soldier's prompt reply to him rebuffs him by saying that is more than they know, implying they are just following orders. A second soldier steps into the chat by stating that 'we know enough if we know we are the king's subjects. If his cause be wrong, our obedience to the king wipes the crime out of us'. Henry tries to refute their views and strolls away pondering all that he has heard, reflecting on the sense of responsibility he carries in his role as the leader of the nation. Historically Henry V was in war of his own making arising from territorial greed and prestige of which his soldiers were in total ignorance, and they had no idea whether the king was right or wrong. They believed that because he was the king they were at the final judgement free of condemnation because the king was responsible.

This sense of obeying orders has been assumed safe at every level of human life. Governments expect their laws to be obeyed, the military to follow their policies, military commanders in turn expect soldiers to obey orders thereby doing their duty. Even in civilian life the same lines of thought are pursued when the foreman tells sacked workers that he is only following the orders of the bosses. The Nuremberg Trials arrived at the belief that criminal and immoral orders should not be obeyed, ignoring the fact of the legal *tu quoque* argument 'that you did the same thing'. Every nation, even the genuine liberal democratic ones, expect orders to be obeyed especially in the trauma of war emergencies. More sensitive souls may have serious qualms, and in times of war pacifists were not welcomed. It is true that some people behave like robots and do what they are told. The psychologist Stanley Milgram in his well-known experiments with electric shocks tried to demonstrate that ordinary people could inflict powerful electric charges on others, simply because an authoritative figure in charge of the experiment informed them it was correct to follow orders.[1] These individuals were seemingly turned into the puppets of their controllers.

Von Senger was highly educated, intelligent, and deeply religious, consequently, the question of how he could serve such an evil regime must be asked. He seems to have turned to his revered 'St Thomas Aquinas, whose creed was', he wrote in his diary, that 'no one can be blamed for the crimes of others in so far as he has no influence over them', then adding the power was not in the hands of the generals.[2] He was a devout Catholic with strong ethical convictions and critical of the regime, but as a patriotic minded German felt obliged to serve his country. He addressed this inner conflict many times, but he continued to the last days of the war to fight for the Nazi regime. He had refused to carry out Hitler's direct order by not executing Italian officers who had followed their government's orders of switching sides, and ignored many other immoral orders, but continued to serve. In doing this he put his life at risk, placed his sense of Christian morality first and foremost, but still served a tyrant.

It has been suggested that he had like others taken the Hitler oath of loyalty, but how he took the oath seriously can only be open to speculation. Manstein wrote that 'officers who were brought up as Christians, and this was the vast majority, particularly in the older generation could not break their oath to their supreme commander, let alone kill him'.[3] Von Senger, who was a Benedictine Oblate and a man not prone to lying, wrote 'how little officers knew of the criminal nature of the Nazi leadership'.[4] It has been claimed that German military tradition put great emphasis on 'the oath', their English equivalents swore allegiance to the monarch, and 'did not differ significantly from that required of civil servants … or by United States army officers to the President'.[5] It should be noted, however, that the oath was deeply personal to Adolf Hitler, whereas the other countries mentioned implied the loyalty was to the state, not one man called Adolf. The fact that von Senger was an ardent Catholic Christian, not just by name or tradition, but by deliberate choice, undoubtedly meant his commitment to his faith was more important than any oath sworn to Adolf Hitler. He 'was one of a growing number of anti-Nazi generals who fought not for a regime they despised but for the honour of Germany'.[6] The general impression is that von Senger comes across as what might be described as an old-fashioned patriot serving his country, not a nationalist. The phrase 'My country right or wrong' springs to mind, it was first expressed, it is believed, by Stephen Decatur about 1820 expressing his loyalty to the United States. It was later changed by Carl Schurz in 1972, who paraphrased that the 'country should be kept right when right and put right when wrong', which would have appealed to von Senger.

For von Senger 'a soldier's honour and loyalty were for him only thinkable in terms of Christian morality and Christian ethics'.[7] He stands out in this belief even when military matters seemed to be in Germany's favour, but as Hitler's military leadership became suspect and Nazi barbarism became apparent, 'a growing number of anti-Nazi generals who fought not for a regime they despised but for the honour of Germany' came to light.[8] Many such Germans were more prompted to turn against Hitler because of the military failures, but 'throughout his career von Senger's pragmatism and humanity were often at odds with the Establishment'.[9]

The question may be asked as to why he was not in the German resistance who were plotting for Hitler's downfall. He knew many of the resisters, admired many of them, had personal acquaintance with some, was aware of the plotting, but he kept his distance. He would often talk to his trusted subordinates about his views on the Nazi leadership, of the inevitability of defeat, and the various evils of the regime, but talk on the resistance he prohibited. It was known by the Nazi hierarchy that he was critical of the regime, and they were deeply suspicious of him. It was later believed that it was Kesselring who saved both von Senger and General Westphal from being interrogated by the Gestapo following the 20 July Plot.

The question could be asked whether his personal ethics were against assassination of the head of state, or that he was worried about being involved. It must remain pure speculation, but having pursued von Senger's life and character what tends to emerge is his intelligent pragmatic approach that it would never work, as it was not just a matter of killing Hitler but bringing down the entire Nazi machine. In this he was right in his judgement, noting that only a final defeat would resolve the problem. After the 20 July Plot he ignored the commands on how to tell the soldiers the plot had failed and never even mentioned the subject as if it were of little consequence. After the 20 July Plot the authorities had expected all military commanders should 'show publicly their jubilation that the Führer had survived and voice frenzied castigation of the culprits'.[10] But he ignored the whole issue entirely when in front of his troops.

There are naturally, and understandably, those who might see von Senger's anti-Nazi approach as being a form of personal postwar defence, but there are many witnesses who often refer to his anti-Nazi views both during the conflict and many recalling them postwar. An Italian general recalled after the war that he had said to von Senger that Clausewitz had once said when defeat was certain peace should be negotiated, von Senger had 'nodded but added that he was sure Hitler had not read Clausewitz – a statement that in Nazi eyes would have been defeatist if not outright treasonous'.[11] As one historian noted, the fact that he claimed postwar that he had been anti-Hitler could be seen as a typical postwar attempt at whitewashing, but in von Senger's case 'the testimony of fellow officers seemed to confirm his anti-Nazi opinions, though not necessarily

Germany's defeat'.[12] It may be concluded that von Senger never lost sight of his Christian morality, that he was strongly against the Nazi regime, but not his country which he served even under the appalling circumstances of the day, making him a man of formidable courage.

Throughout his personal account it is clear that he felt a high degree of personal angst, that many Germans from all social classes and levels of education, had failed to understand the moral depravity of the Nazi leadership. This thought undoubtedly called into mind his own belief that he was serving the state as his father had influenced him. Although he was guilt-free of obeying criminal orders and not behaving in an immoral fashion, speculatively, it is easy to understand that he had serious doubts about serving the Nazi regime. He, as noted in the main body of the text, knew that effective opposition was impossible, and in his final paragraph asked the question as to 'how could so many Germans shut their eyes to all these wretched aberrations and crimes?'[13] He raised the question that even the more intelligent people had seen the weaknesses of the Weimar democracy and had therefore approved of a firm leadership, and Hitler's early successes had seemed to confirm this aspect. He did not raise the issue that the German people had been hoodwinked, as in 1930–33 Hitler's Nazi Party (NSDAP) were constantly mentioning a better future, more employment, more money, and better living conditions. There was no mention of war or genocide. It was probably the case that he was looking for something better than the crumbling Weimar Republic, but it did not take him long to detect the Nazi criminality and immorality. He tried to make some rethink their views, and discovered their knowledge was badly limited. He stood back as it dawned on him that the more knowledgeable ones bore more responsibility than those who were ignorant, thereby assuming the Nazi regime, because it was the government, had been right. He also pondered why some nations had experienced successful dictatorship and seemed to have flourished even though they allowed no political freedom which raises his political views.

Political Outlook

When Hitler came to power in 1939, his daughter said, 'He had to go or stay, and he believed that in spite of Hitler he should remain with his people'.[14] His father had instilled in him that the family served the state, and the state was the people. This was meaningful to a man like von Senger, a member of the old minor aristocracy who felt a responsibility for the people in general. As one historian wrote, 'He had indeed served Hitler's state loyally. Within the sphere of his own commands, he had permitted not one deviation from the accepted code of Christian morality. It was the state, not its Führer, that he had served; he was never one of Hitler's generals'.[15]

His political outlook was astute and after the defeat of France it dawned on him that even those Germans who had held suspicions about Hitler became less critical of him and even more trusting. He was correct because many Germans had rejoiced in the downfall if France, often seen as their traditional enemy, and who had rigorously enforced the humiliating terms of the Versailles Treaty. Many of the military men who had been suspicious also rapidly changed their minds. Keitel described Hitler as 'he who is above reproach of any lack of dash and daring' as innocent, underlining as with many others that at this stage with victory after victory, Hitler was almost deified as a military genius. Von Senger, however, despite the victory could see how it helped boost public support for the Nazi regime he already distrusted, the news of the Polish atrocities having been brought to his attention. Later, after witnessing firsthand the Russian war on the Stalingrad front, he concluded that for him and those like him who retained their distrust, it appeared that only a military defeat would rid Germany of this government. He never changed his mind on this view although as a servant of his country, he continued in a war he knew was lost. In Italy von Senger often said to his aide, 'the rotten thing is to keep on fighting and fighting and to know also that we have lost this war'.[16]

He was no fool, and he selected the right people with whom to share his views. 'None of the men Senger chose would report their chief for defeatist talk'.[17] He would often sit with his officers and discuss the ups and downs of the war, only the resistance against Hitler was never mentioned. He often had similar discussions with some Italian military whom he befriended, and his very actions would have indicated to them where von Senger stood in these matters. As noted, many times his views although shared with those he trusted, were widely known by the Nazi hierarchy, and he was probably left alone because after successfully extracting German troops from the major Mediterranean islands off Italy, and putting up such a stout defence in Cassino, he was recognised as a reliable battlefield general. When he met Hitler, von Senger was very aware that the Führer was distrustful of him, and he was sent packing to a Nazi indoctrination course. It would have been no surprise that when the so-called Hitler Line looked in danger, the Führer demanded its name should be changed to avoid embarrassment, the new name being the Senger Line.[18] Given the Nazi reaction to internal opposition, and especially after the 20 July Plot that von Senger survived to write his accounts, and when Clark accepted the surrender of the German Armies in Italy it was von Senger who was the German representative. 'It is fair to conclude that von Senger's military successes were the only reason he escaped OKW retribution for his repeated defiance of orders he considered illegal and immoral'.[19]

There is no question that like many Germans and other nations, von Senger had a distaste for the Bolsheviks as he did for Hitler and worried what the future shape of Europe would be. This political concern explains why he probably helped the postwar Bonn government so much when they re-established their military with Allied help, as the fear of Russia in the Cold War grew. There seems little doubt that at heart he was democratic, but after Hitler not an extreme right-winger nor on the extreme left, and it is easy to deduce with his experience and background he was probably right of centre.

Military side

Having taken on a military role because of the Great War he remained within the system and apart from loving his horses while in the cavalry, and then watching them exchanged for motorised divisions, he developed a strong interest in strategy and tactics, especially the latter as a battlefield commander. Many historians have noted that 'At the heart of von Senger's system of command and control was his concern with standards of training and leadership at all levels. Unlike many Allied commanders, he sought daily contact with those two or three levels below his own immediate subordinates. He made personal reconnaissance of the enemy from forward positions'.[20] He was forever visiting the fighting soldiers on the front line and sharing their dangers. 'Senger's manner as he talked to the men was cheerful, even jovial, especially in contrast to some of his grim fellow generals, but he kept on asking questions till he had the information he wanted'.[21] He would visit the frontline to see his friend General Baade where there was little cover, and the ground was too rocky to dig and build cover from incoming enemy fire and shells. His humanity emerges in the account where he had tea with Baade alongside a shot down British pilot.

He made many personal friends amongst his subordinate officers who obviously liked and trusted him. It was noted that 'In the first weeks of his new assignment [Cassino] Senger spent much of his time getting acquainted with his men and with the terrain in which they would be fighting'.[22] Wandering off in his old Volkswagen and walking the mountains, from which he not only found some enjoyment, but that way he understood the nature of the terrain. The historian Atkinson in his brilliant account of the Italian campaign wrote that von Senger 'stalked the battlefield with his walking stick. Using the Abbey as his pole star, he travelled alone and on foot to be less conspicuous – an adjutant trailed several hundred yards behind the corps commander – and always in daylight, to see as much as possible'.[23] The ordinary soldiers as in any army would have appreciated seeing their commander with them, sharing the danger. Quite what they thought about him when he closed the brothels in Bologna and gave them Opera tickets instead needs little speculation.

He had already established a sound military reputation as 'the (anti-Nazi) Senger had commanded the withdrawal of German troops from Sicily, Sardinia and Corsica, and was a master of the rearguard action'.[24] He embedded this reputation of being a reliable commander in his well-known defence of Cassino. One historian noting 'the purpose of the Germans' stubborn defence in the mountains to the south, conducted with great skill by General von Senger, was to deal with the advancing Allies while they prepared to use the Monte Cassino barrier to its fullest effect'.[25] They would fight corner by corner then back to the next one, with the Allies having to clear mined roads. His tactics, for which he was becoming well known, were carefully thought through, using the nature of the terrain, and watching the enemy which brought devastation on the Americans at the Rapido river battle. Atkinson noted that 'no man contributed more to Allied miseries at San Pietro, the Rapido River, and Cassino than von Senger'.[26] However, von Senger was no illusionist and knew he would lose but fought on to achieve what he knew could be an inevitable delay to the Allied forces. The enemy who opposed him in Italy recognised his skills, and the British military historian Liddell Hart described von Senger as an 'able commander'.[27] After the war and imprisonment von Senger would start a new career in education, but the Bonn government used his military experience, not least in selecting the right personnel to be officers, indicating his military reputation lived on.

The Man von Senger

Von Senger cared for people whatever their rank and whoever they were. This was clearly evidenced with the care for his soldiers, worrying about their safety and even their comfort. In the midst of the Cassino battle he organised a 'seat barrow' for wounded men so four stretcher bearers were not in danger, and 'he moved the field kitchens closer to the lines and had the food containers insulated with straw' so the food arrived hot.[28] He knew that in the end it would be a lost war, but in his history of the Second World War Max Hastings, who only mentions him once, wrote that 'von Senger, a rare and indisputable good German, soldiered on like the professional he was'.[29] As he pursued his work he met and talked with civilians as an equal, and in his usual friendly fashion in occupied France ate and drank with other customers in a café, and even stopped to chat with Italian farmworkers. It was not just charm but an interest in those caught up in the war. His aide Cramm recalled that he followed the request of a priest and interceded with the SS to free some of their civilian hostages.[30] His love of the churches and religious bodies such as nunneries and monasteries was well known, and it has been suggested by von Senger and several historians the Italian partisans posed no threat to him personally because of his good will towards the Italian people, even when they switched sides.

He must have struck people who saw him more as a strange character for a German general, and in the Cassino area von Senger ' had rambled across these hills, swinging his six-foot ashplant [walking stick], his loping gait said to resemble a sailor's more than a soldier's, often chatting up peasants in his passable, lisping Italian'.[31] Kesselring was known as 'smiling Albert' because many photographs show him looking amenable, but of all the German generals von Senger was most probably the most friendly and affable with strangers and soldiers alike.

He was a courageous man, not just because he spent more time on the frontline with his soldiers than most other commanders, his hatred of Nazism he barely disguised. He had a 'personality rooted in the concept of duty, Christian morality, with the world-wide outlook of a convinced liberal democrat'.[32] It has been claimed that 'Senger, in retrospect, stands out as one of the most extraordinary of Hitler's generals…more at home talking history or music …he looked and acted more like an intellectual than one of Hitler's generals.'[33]

He was no saint, but for his post as a German general in the Nazi era he was an unusually decent and pleasant human being. This view can be supported by the number of people who appreciated and liked him, confirmed by available data and observations by military historians. His subordinate officers and soldiers knew he cared for their welfare, and although the Nazi hierarchy were aware of his distaste for them, he was never, as far is known, denounced, or informed on. He made lifelong friends among the Italians and French people even though he had been a member of the occupying forces, staying in touch with them during the postwar years. He eventually failed in protecting the Monte Cassino Abbey because of the overwhelming odds, even allowing his soldiers to occupy the slope virtually up to the walls, which he did for sound military reasons and caring for men in his charge. Nevertheless, the Italian Church recognised his efforts and attitudes, and to this day still condemn the Allies for the bombing, while recognising von Senger's efforts to preserve their heritage as they did with Kesselring. He had helped and befriended the nuns, he was known to have rescued civilians from the clutches of the SS and for caring about ordinary people caught up in the mayhem of war, all of which was simply unusual. He spent years in prison but was never charged or associated with any war crime and was used by his captors to help in various positions. While in the Bridgend PoW camp he made lifelong friends of men like Liddell Hart and Kurt Hahn, and he was even allowed to wander out of the camp and invited by locals to visit a local hunt. It was after one of these outings when he was returning to camp, that it was an ordinary sentry who told him he had been released.

This study during its exploration made every effort not to be a hagiography and acknowledged he was no saint. However, in a world war torn apart by hatred and revenge he offered a glimmer of hope because of his sense of fairness and care for others, friend, and foe, not just a curious but an extremely unusual German general who based his actions on his Christian belief backed by his intellect and humanity.

Notes

Introduction

1. Graham, D. & Bidwell, S., *Tug of War: The Battle for Italy 1943–45* (Yorkshire: Pen & Sword, 2004), p.166.
2. Ibid., p.143.
3. Ibid., p.336.
4. D'Este, Carlo, *Fatal Decision: Anzio and the Battle for Rome* (London: Fontana, 1991), p.90.
5. Ibid.
6. Graham, D. & Bidwell, S., *Tug of War: The Battle for Italy 1943–45*, p.167.
7. Ibid.

Chapter 1

1. Hapgood, David & Richardson, David, *Monte Cassino* (London: Angus & Robertson, 1984), p.42.
2. Von Senger und Etterlin, General Frido, *Neither Fear nor Hope* (London: MacDonald, 1963), p.42.
3. Von Senger, *Neither Fear nor Hope*, p.19.
4. See Porch, Douglas, *Hitler's Mediterranean Gamble: The North African and the Mediterranean Campaigns in World War II* (London: Weidenfeld & Nicolson, 2004), p.508.
5. Trulli, Giuseppe, *Von Senger: U Uomo, Un Generale* (Soldiership, Zanica, 2015), p.10.

Chapter 2

1. Von Senger, *Neither Fear nor Hope*, p.16.
2. Ibid., p.17.
3. Liddell Hart, B.H., *The German Generals Talk* (London: Harper, 2002), p.10.
4. Jeffery, Keith, *MI6: The History of the Intelligence Service 1909–1949* (London: Bloomsbury, 2010), p.295.
5. Von Senger, *Neither Fear nor Hope*, p.27.
6. Hapgood, David & Richardson, David, *Monte Cassino*, p.40.
7. Von Senger, *Neither Fear nor Hope*, p.37.
8. Moseley, Ray, *Mussolini's Shadow: The Double Life of Count Galeazzo Ciano* (London: Yale University Press, 1999), p.91.
9. Ciano's Diary, (Ed) De Felice, Renzo, *Ciano's Diary 1937–1943* (London: Phoenix Press, 2002), p.318.
10. Thomas, R.T., *Britain and Vichy: The Dilemma of Anglo-French Relations 1940–1942* (London: Macmillan, 1979), p.5.
11. Jackson, Julian, *France: The Dark Years 1940–1944* (Oxford: OUP, 2003), p.179.
12. Von Senger, *Neither Fear nor Hope*, p.60.
13. Ibid., p.61.
14. Von Senger und Etterlin, Fridolin von, Liaison Activities with Italian 6th Army. Foreign Military Studies MS at C-095. Headquarters, U.S. Army Europe: Historical Division. (C-095 refers to *War Diary of the Italian Campaign (1943–45)* by General to der Panzertruppen Frido von Senger und Etterlin; 8 vols, p.499, 1951).
15. Von Senger, *Neither Fear nor Hope*, p.79.
16. Ibid., p.95.
17. Ibid., p.99.

18. Ibid., p.102.
19. Ibid., p.105.

Chapter 3

1. Liddell Hart, B.H., *History of the Second World War* (London: Book Club Associates, 1973), p.436.
2. D'Este, Carlo, *Fatal Decision*, p.22.
3. Trevor-Roper, Hugh (Ed.), *Hitler's War Directives* (London: Pan Books, 2004), pp.297–8.
4. KNA, Top-Secret-Cypher-Telegram/19-March-45, Ref/FO-954/ 17A-File, Re-296.
5. Von Senger, *Neither Fear nor Hope*, p.152.
6. D'Este, Carlo, *Fatal Decision*, p.22.
7. Kesselring, Albert, *The Memoirs of Field-Marshal Kesselring* (London: William Kimber, 1953), p.158.
8. Muggeridge, M. (Ed), *Ciano's Diary*, p.393.
9. Capa, Robert, *Slightly out of Focus* (New York: Modern Library, 1999), p.70.
10. Bradley, Omar N., *A General's Life* (London: Sidgwick & Jackson, 1983), p.180.
11. See Atkinson, Rick, *The Day of the Battle: The War in Sicily and Italy 1943–1944* (London: Abacus, 2013), p.115.
12. See Von Senger, *Neither Fear nor Hope*, p.152.
13. DDI, Mussolini to Hitler, 12 July 1943, *DDI* 9 X, pp.647ff. *KTB OKW* Vol. 6, p.771. Santoni, *Le operazioni in Sicilia e Calabria*, pp.223ff.
14. Von Senger, *Neither Fear nor Hope*, p.132.
15. Blumenson, Martin (Ed.), *The Patton Papers 1940–1945* (New York: Da Capo Press, 1996), p.283.
16. Porch, Douglas, *Hitler's Mediterranean Gamble*, p.428.
17. Von Senger, *Neither Fear nor Hope*, p.129.
18. Kesselring, Albert, *The Memoirs of Field-Marshal Kesselring*, p.164.
19. Hastings, Max, *All Hell Let Loose* (London: Harper, 2011), p.450.
20. Stewart, Adrian, *The Campaigns of Alexander of Tunis 1940–45* (Barnsley: Pen & Sword Military, 2008), p.120.
21. Von Senger, *Neither Fear nor Hope*, p.159.
22. Lamb, Richard, *War in Italy, 1943–1945* (London: Murray, 1993), p.179.
23. Ibid., p.180.
24. Von Senger, *Neither Fear nor Hope*, p.162.
25. D'Este, Carlo, *Fatal Decision*, p.86.
26. Bradley, Omar N., *A General's Life*, p.161 and Alexander Earl of Tunis, *The Alexander Memoirs 1940–1945* (London: Frontline Books, 2010), p.125.
27. Eisenhower, Dwight D., *Crusade in Europe* (London: Heinemann, 1948), p.207 and Alexander, *The Alexander Memoirs 1940–1945*, p.109.
28. *The Times*, 31 December 1943.

Chapter 4

1. See Hapgood, David & Richardson, David, *Monte Cassino*, p.45.
2. Dandeker, C., *Surveillance, Power, and Modernity* (London: Polity Press, 1990), pp.82–3.
3. Faulkner, N., Military History, *The Second Front* (Issue 38, November 2013), p.27.
4. Lewis, J. (Ed.), *World War II: The Autobiography* (London: Robinson, 2009), p.448.
5. Hapgood, David & Richardson, David, *Monte Cassino*, p.38.
6. Eisenhower, Dwight D., *Crusade in Europe*, p.157.
7. Roberts, Andrew, *The Storm of War: A New History of the Second World War* (London: Allen Lane, 2009), p.312.
8. Eisenhower, Dwight D., *Crusade in Europe*, p.163.
9. Sangster, Andrew, *Alan Brooke: Churchill's Right-hand Critic* (Oxford & Philadelphia: Casemate, 2020), p.210.
10. Harper, G. & Tonkin-Covell, J., *The Battles of Monte Cassino: The Campaign and its Controversies* (Auckland: Allen & Unwin, 2013), p.92.

11. Ellis, John, *Cassino: The Hollow Victory – The Battle for Rome, January-June 1944* (London: Sphere Books, 1985), p.32.
12. Ibid., p.163.
13. Majdalany, Fred, *The Battle of Cassino* (London: White Lion Publishers, 1973, first published by Longmans, 1957), p.37.
14. Porch, Douglas, *Hitler's Mediterranean Gamble*, p.509.
15. D'Este, Carlo, *Fatal Decision*, p.144.
16. Harper, G. & Tonkin-Covell, J., *The Battles of Monte Cassino*, p.174.
17. Ibid., p.177.
18. Mikolashek, Jon B., *General Mark Clark: Commander of U.S. Fifth Army and Liberator of Rome* (Oxford: Casemate, 2013), p.85.
19. Clark, General Mark, *Papers*, The Citadel Archives and Museum, Charleston. Accessed via The Citadel Archives Digital Collections (omeka.net), 20 January 1944.
20. Walker, Fred L., *From Texas to Rome: A General's Journal* (Dallas: Taylor Publishing Co, 1969), p.296.
21. Ibid., p.305.
22. Ibid., p.310.
23. Mikolashek, Jon B., *General Mark Clark*, p.89.
24. Clark, General Mark, *Papers*, 21 January 1944.
25. Mikolashek, Jon B., *General Mark Clark*, p.90.
26. Ibid., p.217.
27. Trevelyan, Raleigh, *Rome '44: The Battle for the Eternal City* (London: Pimlico, 2004), p.50.
28. D'Este, Carlo, *Fatal Decision*, p.404.
29. Knight, Nigel, *Churchill: The Greatest Briton Unmasked* (Cincinnati: David and Charles Ltd, 2009), p.251.
30. Harper, G. & Tonkin-Covell, J., *The Battles of Monte Cassino*, p.7.
31. Detweiler, Burdick, Rohwer (Eds), *German Military Studies WWII, Kesselring's remarks on Med Campaign 4 July 1948* Vol 14 (London: Garland, 1979), pp.3–4.
32. Porch, Douglas, *Hitler's Mediterranean Gamble*, p.522.
33. Atkinson, Rick, *The Day of the Battle*, p.432.
34. Hodges, Richard, 'Tempting Providence: The Bombing of Monte Cassino' in *History Today* (Volume 44, Issue 2, 1994).
35. Carver, Tom, *Where the Hell Have you Been? Monty, Italy and One Man's Incredible Escape* (London: Short Books, 2009), p.144.
36. Alexander Earl of Tunis, *The Alexander Memoirs 1940–1945*, pp.119–20.
37. Westphal, Siegfried, *The German Army in the West* (London: Cassell, 1951), p.155.
38. Hodges, Richard, 'Tempting Providence: The Bombing of Monte Cassino' in *History Today*, p.246.
39. Von Senger, *Neither Fear nor Hope*, p.187.
40. Harper, G. & Tonkin-Covell, J., *The Battles of Monte Cassino*, p.35.
41. Ibid., p.36.
42. Hodges, Richard, 'Tempting Providence: The Bombing of Monte Cassino' in *History Today* (Volume 44, Issue 2, 1994).
43. Vassiltchikov, Marie, *The Berlin Diaries 1940–45* (London: Pimlico, 1999), p.151.
44. *The Times*, 20 April 1944, p.3.
45. Kesselring, Albert, *The Memoirs of Field-Marshal Kesselring*, p.195.
46. Von Senger, *Neither Fear nor Hope*, p.202.
47. Harper, G. & Tonkin-Covell, J., *The Battles of Monte Cassino*, p.54.
48. Atkinson, Rick, *The Day of the Battle*, p.439.
49. Ellis, John, *Cassino: The Hollow Victory*, p.406.
50. Hodges, Richard, 'Tempting Providence: The Bombing of Monte Cassino' in *History Today*.
51. Harper, G. & Tonkin-Covell, J., *The Battles of Monte Cassino*, pp.52–3.
52. D'Este, Carlo, *Fatal Decision*, p.260.
53. Hapgood, David & Richardson, David, *Monte Cassino*, p.90.
54. Harper, G. & Tonkin-Covell, J., *The Battles of Monte Cassino*, p.50.
55. Atkinson, Rick, *The Day of the Battle*, p.453.

56. Salmaggi, C. & Pallavisini, A., *2194 Days of War: An Illustrated Chronology of the Second World War* (Milan: Galley Press, 1977), p.498.
57. Harper, G. & Tonkin-Covell, J., *The Battles of Monte Cassino*, p.149.
58. Ellis, John, *Cassino: The Hollow Victory*, p.20.
59. Harper, G. & Tonkin-Covell, J., *The Battles of Monte Cassino*, p.144.
60. Ibid., p.92.
61. Ellis, John, *Cassino: The Hollow Victory*, p.32.
62. Harper, G. & Tonkin-Covell, J., *The Battles of Monte Cassino*, p.163.
63. Ibid., p.99.
64. Molony, C.J.C.; Flynn, F.C.; Davies, H.L. & Gleave, T.P., *The Mediterranean and Middle East, Volume V* (London: HMSO, 1973), p.386.
65. Keegan, J., *The Second World War* (London: Arrow Books, 1990), p.359 and stated by Montgomery and quoted in Harper & Tonkin-Covell, *The Battles of Monte Cassino*, p.105. Alexander and Wilson did not get on, Harper, G. & Tonkin-Covell, J., *The Battles of Monte Cassino*, p.110.
66. Ellis, John, *Cassino: The Hollow Victory*, p.475.
67. Von Senger, *Neither Fear nor Hope*, p.201.
68. Nicholas, Lynn, *The Rape of Europa: The Fate of Europe's Treasures in the Third Reich and the Second World War* (London: Papermac, 1995), p.239.
69. Nicholas, Lynn, *The Rape of Europa*, p.241.
70. Atkinson, Rick, *The Day of the Battle*, p.399.
71. Militärgeschichtliches Forschungsamt Potsdam (Eds), *Germany and the Second World War, Volume IX/X* (Oxford: Clarendon, 2001), p.907.
72. Recorded in Trulli, Giuseppe, *Von Senger*, p.139.
73. Nicholas, Lynn, *The Rape of Europa*, p.241.
74. Ibid., p.244.
75. Weizsäcker, Ernst von, *Memoirs* (London: Gollanz, 1951), p.293.
76. Von Senger, *Neither Fear nor Hope*, p.203.
77. Ibid., p.206.
78. Porch, Douglas, *Hitler's Mediterranean Gamble*, p.533.
79. Majdalany, Fred, *The Battle of Cassino*, pp.46 and 91.
80. Von Senger, *Neither Fear nor Hope*, p.227.
81. Ibid.
82. Von Senger, *Neither Fear nor Hope*, p.231.
83. Atkinson, Rick, *The Day of the Battle*, p.451.
84. *Independent* Newspaper, 3 October 2006, article revealed Maxwell under investigation for war crimes.
85. Von Senger, *Neither Fear nor Hope*, p.242.
86. Westphal, Siegfried, *The German Army in the West*, p.166.
87. D'Este, Carlo, *Fatal Decision*, p.404.
88. Westphal, Siegfried, *The German Army in the West*, p.156.
89. Schellenberg, Walter, *Schellenberg* (London: Mayflower, 1965), p.157–8.
90. Grace, Edward, *The Perilous Road to Rome & Beyond* (Yorkshire: Pen & Sword, 2007).
91. Trevelyan, Raleigh, *Rome '44*, p.192 and Kesselring, Albert, *The Memoirs of Field-Marshal Kesselring*, p.196.
92. Kesselring, Albert, *The Memoirs of Field-Marshal Kesselring*, p.198.
93. Knight, Nigel, *Churchill*, p.251.
94. Atkinson, Rick, *The Day of the Battle*, p.524.
95. Von Senger, *Neither Fear nor Hope*, p.250.
96. Trevelyan, Raleigh, *Rome '44*, p.288.
97. Porch, Douglas, *Hitler's Mediterranean Gamble*, pp.422–3.
98. Trevelyan, *Rome '44*, p.381.
99. Clark, General Mark, *Calculated Risk* (New York: Enigma Books, 2007), p.332.
100. D'Este, Carlo, *Fatal Decision*, p.365.
101. Ibid., p.68.
102. Ibid., p.58.

103. Graham, D. & Bidwell, S., *Tug of War: The Battle for Italy 1943–45*, p.315.
104. Whicker, Alan, *Whicker's War* (London: Harpers, 2005), p.183.
105. Hastings, Max, *All Hell Let Loose*, pp.454–5.
106. Ibid., p.530.
107. Alexander, *The Alexander Memoirs 1940–1945*, p.125.
108. Ibid.
109. Hastings, Max, *All Hell Let Loose*, p.529.
110. Von Senger, *Neither Fear nor Hope*, p.254.
111. Ibid., p.256.
112. Ibid., p.266.
113. Kesselring, Albert, *The Memoirs of Field-Marshal Kesselring*, p.209.
114. Dollmann, Eugen, *The Interpreter: Memoirs of Doktor Eugen Dollmann* (London: Hutchinson, 1967), p.330.
115. Macksey, Kenneth, *Kesselring: German Master Strategist of the Second World War* (London: Greenhill, 1978), p.217.
116. Ibid.
117. Dollmann, Eugen, *The Interpreter*, p.330.
118. Von Senger, *Neither Fear nor Hope*, p.274.
119. Ibid., p.277.
120. Hassell, Ulrich von, *The Ulrich von Hassell Diaries: The Story of the Forces Against Hitler Inside Germany* (London: Frontline Books, 2011), pp.12 and 196.
121. Von Senger, *Neither Fear nor Hope*, p.291.
122. D'Este, Carlo, *Fatal Decision*, p.427.

Chapter 5

1. Davies, Norman, *No Simple Victory: World War II in Europe, 1939–1945* (London: Penguin, 2007), p.303.
2. Westphal, Siegfried, *The German Army in the West*, pp.55–6.
3. Toland, John, *The Last 100 Days* (New York: Modern Library, 2003), p.238.
4. Macmillan, Harold, *The Blast of War: 1939–1945* (London: Macmillan, 1967), p.707.
5. Dollmann, Eugen, *The Interpreter*, p.333.
6. Bundesarchiv-Militärarchiv, Freiburg: N574–19, 'Kriegsende in Italien' pp.53–4; & Kershaw, Ian, *The End: Hitler's Germany* (London: Allen Lane, 2011), p.364.
7. Kershaw, Ian, *The End*, p.396.
8. Hassell, Ulrich von, *The Von Hassell Diaries* (London: Hamish Hamilton, 1948), p.272.
9. KNA-HW1/3007.
10. Kurzman, Dan, *A Special Mission: Hitler's Secret Plot to Seize the Vatican and Kidnap Pope Pius XII* (New York: Da Capo Press, 2007), p.238.
11. Clark, General Mark, *Calculated Risk*, p.346.
12. Ibid., p.346.
13. Ibid., p.347.
14. Ibid., p.347.
15. Raiber, Richard, *Anatomy of Perjury: Field Marshal Albert Kesselring, Via Rasella, and the GINNY Mission* (Delaware: Delaware Press, 2008), p.104.
16. Atkinson, Rick, *The Day of the Battle*, p.499.
17. Von Senger, *Neither Fear nor Hope*, p.344.
18. LRWC-Vol-1, *Dostler Case*, p.8, The UN War Crimes Commission, (1949) *Law-Reports of Trials of War Criminals, Volume VIII*, London; Volume VIII Case No 47, London: *Law Reports of Trials of War Criminals.*
19. Raiber, Richard, *Anatomy of Perjury*, p.169.
20. Ibid., p.170.
21. Ibid., p.171.
22. Ibid., p.178.
23. Bower, Tom, *Blind Eye to Murder* (London: Little Brown & Co, 1981), p.244.
24. Von Senger, *Neither Fear nor Hope*, p.349.
25. Ibid., p.350.

26. See Liddell Hart Centre for Military Archives, King's College, London. Reference Code 9/24/79.
27. Liddell Hart, B.H., *The Other Side of the Hill* (London: Pan Books, 1978), p.332.
28. Ibid., p.345.
29. See Liddell Hart Centre for Military Archives, King's College, London. Reference Code 9/24/138.
30. Von Senger, *Neither Fear nor Hope*, p.354.
31. Bradley, Omar N., *A General's Life*, p.159.
32. Alexander, *The Alexander Memoirs 1940–1945*, p.159.
33. Von Senger, *Neither Fear nor Hope*, p.339.

Chapter 6

1. Trulli, Giuseppe, *Von Senger, U Uomo, Un Generale* (Soldiership, Zanica, 2015).
2. See Klemperer, Victor, *The Lesser Evil: The Diaries of Victor Klemperer 1945–1959* translated by Martin Chalmers (London: Phoenix an imprint of Orion Books, 2004).
3. Air Historical Branch, Translation No. VII/166, *Liaison Activities with Italian 6th Army – A Postwar study by General von Senger und Etterlin, with Comments by Generals Halder and Mueller-Hillebrand.* Translated by A.H.B.6, Air Ministry, September 1957.

Chapter 7

1. See Milgram, Stanley, *Obedience to Authority: An Experimental View* (New York: Harper and Row, 1974).
2. D'Este, Carlo, *Fatal Decision*, p.89.
3. Mungo, Melvin, *Manstein: Hitler's Greatest General* (London: Weidenfeld & Nicolson, 2010), p.435.
4. Von Senger, *Neither Fear nor Hope*, p.296.
5. Tipton, Frank B., *A History of Modern Germany Since 1815* (London: Continuum, 2003), p.427.
6. D'Este, Carlo, *Fatal Decision*, p.89.
7. Barnett, Correlli (Ed.), *Hitler's Generals* (New York: Grove Weidenfeld, 1989), p.376.
8. D'Este, Carlo, *Fatal Decision*, p.89.
9. Ibid., p.90.
10. Barnett, Correlli (Ed.), *Hitler's Generals*, p.387.
11. Hapgood, David & Richardson, David, *Monte Cassino*, p.40.
12. Ibid., p.41.
13. Von Senger, *Neither Fear nor Hope*, p.339.
14. Hapgood, David & Richardson, David, *Monte Cassino*, p.40.
15. Barnett, Correlli (Ed.), *Hitler's Generals*, p.389.
16. Hapgood, David & Richardson, David, *Monte Cassino*, p.174.
17. Ibid.
18. See Atkinson, Rick, *The Day of the Battle*, p.533.
19. D'Este, Carlo, *Fatal Decision*, p.427.
20. Barnett, Correlli (Ed.), *Hitler's Generals*, p.385.
21. Hapgood, David & Richardson, David, *Monte Cassino*, p.38.
22. Ibid., p.44.
23. Atkinson, Rick, *The Day of the Battle*, p.468.
24. Roberts, Andrew, *The Storm of War*, p.386.
25. Hapgood, David & Richardson, David, *Monte Cassino*, p.38.
26. Atkinson, Rick, *The Day of the Battle*, p.435.
27. Liddell Hart, B.H., *History of the Second World War*, p.534.
28. Hapgood, David & Richardson, David, *Monte Cassino*, p.124.
29. Hastings, Max, *All Hell Let Loose*, p.529.
30. Hapgood, David & Richardson, David, *Monte Cassino*, p.176.
31. Atkinson, Rick, *The Day of the Battle*, p.435.
32. Barnett, Correlli (Ed.), *Hitler's Generals*, p.381.
33. Hapgood, David & Richardson, David, *Monte Cassino*, p.39.

Bibliography

Primary Sources

Air Historical Branch, Translation No. VII/166, *Liaison Activities with Italian 6th Army – A Postwar study by General von Senge und Etterlin, with Comments by Generals Halder and Mueller-Hillebrand.* Translated by A.H.B.6, Air Ministry, September 1957.

Bundesarchiv-Militärarchiv, Freiburg: N574-19, 'Kriegsende in Italien', pp.53–4.

Clark, General Mark, *Papers*, The Citadel Archives and Museum, Charleston. Accessed via The Citadel Archives Digital Collections (omeka.net), 20 January 1944.

DDI, Mussolini to Hitler, 12 July 1943, DDI 9 X, pp.647ff. KTB OKW Vol. 6, p.771. Santoni, *Le operazioni in Sicilia e Calabria*, pp.223ff.

Kew National Archives – KNA, Top-Secret-Cypher-Telegram/19-March-45, Ref/FO-954/17AFile, Re-296. And KNA-HW1/3007.

Liddell Hart Centre for Military Archives, King's College, London. Reference Code 9/24/79.

LRWC-Vol-1, *Dostler Case*, p.8.

The Times, 31 December 1943. .... *The Times*, 20 April 1944 ... *Independent*, 3 October 2006, article revealed Maxwell under investigation for war crimes.

The UN War Crimes Commission (1949), *Law Reports of Trials of War Criminals, Volume VIII*, Case No 47, London.

Von Senger und Etterlin, Fridolin von, Liaison Activities with Italian 6th Army. Foreign Military Studies MS at C-095. Headquarters, U.S. Army Europe: Historical Division. (C-095 refers to War Diary of the Italian Campaign (1943–45) by General to der Panzertruppen Frido von Senger und Etterlin; 8 vols, 499pp; 1951).

Memoirs, Diarists and Biographies

Alexander Earl of Tunis, *The Alexander Memoirs 1940–1945* (London: Frontline Books, 2010)

Bradley, Omar N., *A General's Life* (London: Sidgwick & Jackson, 1983)

Ciano's Diary, (Ed) De Felice, Renzo, *Ciano's Diary 1937–1943* (London: Phoenix Press, 2002)

Ciano's Diary, Muggeridgem, M. (Ed), *Ciano's Diary 1939–1943* (London: William Heinemann, 1947)

Clark, General Mark, *Calculated Risk* (London: Harrup, 1951)

Dollmann, Eugen, *The Interpreter: Memoirs of Doktor Eugen Dollmann* (London: Hutchinson, 1967)

Eisenhower, Dwight D., *Crusade in Europe* (London: Heinemann, 1948)

Hassell, Ulrich von, *The Ulrich von Hassell Diaries: The Story of the Forces Against Hitler Inside Germany* (London: Frontline Books, 2011)

Kesselring, Albert, *The Memoirs of Field-Marshal Kesselring* (London: William Kimber, 1953)

Klemperer, Victor, *The Lesser Evil: The Diaries of Victor Klemperer 1945–1959* translated by Martin Chalmers (London: Phoenix an imprint of Orion Books, 2004)

Macksey, Kenneth, *Kesselring: German Master Strategist of the Second World War* (London: Greenhill, 1978)

Macmillan, Harold, *The Blast of War: 1939–1945* (London: Macmillan, 1967)

Mikolashek, Jon B., *General Mark Clark: Commander of U.S. Fifth Army and Liberator of Rome* (Oxford: Casemate, 2013)

Padfield, Peter, *Himmler: Reichsführer-SS* (London: Cassell & Co, 2001)

Patton Papers 1940–1945, The (edited by Blumenson, Martin) (New York: Da Capo Press, 1996)

Sangster, Andrew, *Alan Brooke: Churchill's Right-hand Critic* (Oxford & Philadelphia: Casemate, 2020)

Schellenberg, Walter, *Schellenberg* (London: Mayflower, 1965)
Trulli, Giuseppe, *Von Senger, U Uomo, Un Generale* (Soldiership, Zanica, 2015)
Vassiltchikov, Marie, *The Berlin Diaries 1940–45* (London: Pimlico, 1999)
Von Senger und Etterlin, General Frido, *Neither Fear nor Hope* (London: MacDonald, 1963)
Weizsäcker, Ernst von, *Memoirs* (London: Gollanz, 1951)
Westphal, Siegfried, *The German Army in the West* (London: Cassell, 1951)
Whicker, Alan, *Whicker's War* (London: Harpers, 2005)

Cited Works

Atkinson, Rick, *The Day of the Battle* (London: Abacus, 2013)
Bower, Tom, *Blind Eye to Murder* (London: Little Brown & Co, 1981)
Capa, Robert *Slightly out of Focus* (New York: Modern Library, 1999)
Carver, Tom, *Where the Hell Have you Been? Monty, Italy and One Man's Incredible Escape* (London: Short Books, 2009)
Barnett, Correlli (Ed.), *Hitler's Generals* (New York: Grove Weidenfeld, 1989)
D'Este, Carlo, *Fatal Decision: Anzio and the Battle for Rome* (London: Fontana, 1991)
Dandeker, C., *Surveillance, Power, and Modernity* (London: Polity Press, 1990)
Davies, Norman, *No Simple Victory: World War II in Europe, 1939–1945* (London: Penguin, 2007)
Detweiler, Burdick, Rohwer (Eds), *German Military Studies WWII, Kesselring's remarks on Med Campaign 4 July 1948* Vol 14 (London: Garland, 1979)
Faulkner, N., Military History, *The Second Front* (Issue 38 November 2013)
Gilbert, Martin, *Winston Churchill: The Wilderness Years* (London: Macmillan, 1981)
Grace, Edward, *The Perilous Road to Rome & Beyond* (Yorkshire: Pen & Sword, 2007).
Graham, D. & Bidwell, S., *Tug of War: The Battle for Italy 1943–45* (Yorkshire: Pen & Sword, 2004)
Hapgood, David & Richardson, David, *Monte Cassino* (London: Angus & Robertson, 1984)
Harper, G. & Tonkin-Covell, J., *The Battles of Monte Cassino: The Campaign and its Controversies* (Auckland: Allen & Unwin, 2013)
Hastings, Max, *All Hell Let Loose* (London: Harper, 2011)
Hodges, Richard, 'Tempting Providence: The Bombing of Monte Cassino' in *History Today* (Volume 44, Issue 2, 1994)
Hoyt, Edwin P., *Backwater War: The Allied Campaign in Italy, 1943–1945* (Mechanicsburg: Stackpole, 2007)
Jackson, Julian, *France: The Dark Years 1940–1944* (Oxford: OUP, 2003)
Jeffery, Keith, *MI6: The History of the Intelligence Service 1909–1949* (London: Bloomsbury, 2010)
Keegan, J., *The Second World War* (London: Arrow Books, 1990)
Kershaw, Ian, *The End: Hitler's Germany* (London: Allen Lane, 2011)
Knight, Nigel, *Churchill: The Greatest Briton Unmasked* (Cincinnati: David and Charles Ltd, 2009)
Kurzman, Dan, *A Special Mission: Hitler's Secret Plot to Seize the Vatican and Kidnap Pope Pius XII* (New York: Da Capo Press, 2007)
Lamb, Richard, *War in Italy 1943–1945* (London: Murray, 1993)
Lewis, J. (Ed.), *World War II: The Autobiography* (London: Robinson, 2009)
Liddell Hart, B.H., *History of the Second World War* (London: Book Club Associates, 1973)
______, *The Other Side of the Hill* (London: Pan Books, 1978)
______, *The German Generals Talk* (London: Harper, 2002)
Majdalany, Fred, *The Battle of Cassino* (London: White Lion Publishers, 1973, first published by Longmans 1957)
Milgram, Stanley, *Obedience to Authority: An Experimental View* (New York: Harper and Row, 1974)
Militärgeschichtliches Forschungsamt Potsdam (Eds), *Germany and the Second World War, Volume IX/X* (Oxford: Clarendon, 2001)
Molony, C.J.C.; Flynn, F.C.; Davies, H.L. & Gleave, T.P., *The Mediterranean and Middle East, Volume V* (London: HMSO, 1973)
Moseley, Ray, *Mussolini's Shadow: The Double Life of Count Galeazzo Ciano* (London: Yale University Press, 1999)
Mungo, Melvin, *Manstein: Hitler's Greatest General* (London: Weidenfeld & Nicolson, 2010)
Nicholas, Lynn, *The Rape of Europa: The Fate of Europe's Treasures in the Third Reich and the Second World War* (London: Papermac, 1995)

Porch, Douglas, *Hitler's Mediterranean Gamble: The North African and the Mediterranean Campaigns in World War II* (London: Weidenfeld & Nicolson, 2004)
Raiber, Richard, *Anatomy of Perjury: Field Marshal Albert Kesselring, Via Rasella, and the GINNY Mission* (Delaware: Delaware Press, 2008)
Roberts, Andrew, *The Storm of War: A New History of the Second World War* (London: Allen Lane, 2009)
Salmaggi, C. & Pallavisini, A., *2194 Days of War: An Illustrated Chronology of the Second World War* (Milan: Galley Press, 1977)
Salter, Michael, *Nazi War Crimes, US Intelligence and Selective Prosecution at Nuremberg* (Oxford: Routledge-Cavendish, 2007)
Stewart, Adrian, *The Campaigns of Alexander of Tunis 1940–45* (Barnsley: Pen & Sword Military, 2008)
Thomas, R.T., *Britain and Vichy: The Dilemma of Anglo-French Relations 1940–1942* (London: Macmillan, 1979)
Tipton, Frank B., *A History of Modern Germany Since 1815* (London: Continuum, 2003)
Toland, John, *The Last 100 Days* (New York: Modern Library, 2003)
Trevelyan, Raleigh, *Rome '44: The Battle for the Eternal City* (London: Pimlico, 2004)
Trevor-Roper, Hugh (Ed.), *Hitler's War Directives* (London: Pan Books, 2004)

Index